I0224769

YOUR
ESSENCE
UNDRESSED
HOW TO DRESS YOUR CONFIDENCE
AND REVEAL THE REAL YOU!
STEFFI JO

Published by Express Your Essence, LLC

www.ExpressYourEssence.com

SteffiJo@ExpressYourEssence.com

ISBN: 978-1-7321615-1-1

Printed in the United States of America

DEDICATION ♥

My first awareness as a child was my love of creating something that others would appreciate, that would bring them joy. My first "business" was making and selling perfumes. I was perhaps six years old, then. I remember looking for scents in anything I could find in the bathroom. I would mix together sweet-smelling shampoos and lotions, gather the little bottles I'd collected, and pour my mixtures in. Instead of making a lemonade stand, I wanted a perfume stand. I was in love with the idea that I could make something, and others might enjoy it enough to buy it!

I dedicate this book to all women who, as little girls, knew they loved to create and knew that someday, what they loved so much would be the driving passion of their own business. For all the women who are creating, emerging, building, and who have become successful doing what they love, this book is written from my heart to yours.

TABLE OF CONTENTS

INTRODUCTION

"It's time to allow the real you the freedom to come out and play!"

—STEFFI JO

Have you ever asked someone, "Does this look good on me?" Most women have asked this question at one time or another. It usually happens when you are not feeling that good about what you are wearing—but you end up walking out the door anyway. You end up feeling…

- Not quite as "put-together" as you would like to be.
- Uncomfortable in social settings, especially when you are just not sure about your appearance.
- Self-conscious about your style. Does it flatter who you are?
- Annoyed by how long it takes for you even to put together an outfit.
- Stressed over picking out the right color for your next event or speaking gig.
- Overwhelmed when shopping for an outfit that shows you off authentically.
- Disconnected because you chose to wear the outfit that was on the mannequin, and you feel awkward when wearing it.

- Like a shopping failure!
- Wasteful with your time and money because of the countless outfits you have bought and have never worn.
- Lost when you walk into your closet; plenty of clothes but nothing to wear!
- Information overload, you know "TMI." There are so many dos & don'ts that you feel you have lost confidence in your choices.
- Just plain stuck in a fog of colors and designs with no direction on how to choose your authentic style and own it?

Your Essence Undressed: How to Dress with Confidence and Reveal the Real You! is for all women who want to feel good about themselves as they show who they are with confidence every day. Stepping outside of the box we have created to fit into when we do not know how to identify our own unique style, our own authentic self. It is the box we get lost within that contains so much information that we forget what aligns with the woman who wants to be seen and acknowledged for her true self.

This book is written for every woman who has stood in her closet with tears in her eyes as she has looked around at her clothes and felt she has nothing to wear. It is a feeling of no identity, a feeling of being lost amidst abundant advice from every direction. This book is for the woman who has had that moment of losing her own meaning and is searching to put herself together with value and integrity that is true to her authentic being. It is for the woman who wishes to be seen in the world for who she is on the inside. Most of all, this book is for the woman who is forever growing and evolving to be the best she can be for herself and others.

I have stood in my closet and cried more than I care to admit until I decided there was more to me and I was going to figure it out. I wanted to be seen and accepted for who I really am and to feel confident in myself again. I would go to the mall and wander in a sea of clothing, seeing many things that were beautiful and trendy, but nothing that felt like it was "me." After browsing racks and spending hours in fitting rooms, I was overwhelmed, drained, and left wondering if I would ever find clothes that not only fit my body but also my style. And what exactly was my style? Things made me look too old or styles that were too young for me to pull off. I bought clothes that never felt totally right because I felt there were no other choices.

I looked around the four walls, with all my clothes hanging and staring back, and I chose to make decisions based on my background of experience that I knew I could pull from to help set me free of this cycle. I knew I was in a state of depression, and the first thing I needed was healing on the inside. If I could at least feel good about the clothes I wore, it would help get me through the day. The thought of using my clothes to help heal me both intrigued me and led me to explore the possibilities that have led me to write this book.

That moment standing in my closet fifteen years ago has changed my life. I hope I can help women open the door to their closet with renewed excitement and awareness of how they can support themselves every day by allowing others to have an experience of who they really are on the inside.

When I decided to explore how to use my clothing as a healing component, I first drew knowledge from who I am as an artist and an empath, my knowledge of healing with color and energy, along with my intuition. I experimented with myself, and I started making sense of who I am underneath all the layers I had covered myself with through the years. I started making sense of the Real me versus the one

I created to hide. I started absorbing any and all information that supported the process of shifting my feelings and thoughts that allowed my true self to become more visible. I began bringing what I was learning to the clothing that I wore; the energy that I was putting on the outside of me would only support me if it aligned with the energy of who I am on the inside.

My clothing was the support of something tangible, something that I needed to help me walk out the door, and it began opening the door to breaking past the depressive thoughts and behaviors. It was enough to get me out the door feeling good about myself, which led to other actions. Sometimes it is just that little step that makes the biggest impact on change.

I have had many teachers along the way, and I have also taught many women along the way. My work has evolved from simply understanding the energy of the clothing we choose to wear and what works best for a person's own unique Essence, into how to understand the nuances of our deepest, purest Essence. It is about how we manifest what we want by being who we are and showing up in our most authentic ways. With the understanding of your unique Essence, you enhance all areas of your life, from everyday living to how you show up at work, how you brand yourself, and how to be with the person in front of you.

NOTICED, SEEN, AND HEARD

In this book, I have chosen to focus on your Essence and how to dress in alignment with the energy of your Essence. This information enhances your authenticity when dressing and presenting yourself in all areas of your life. The results are attracting more of what you want by being more of who you are. You become a walking light beam of attraction. You are noticed, seen, heard, listened to with more interest. People are curious about you; they see the alignment and the authenticity—and they want it, too!

My vision and my passion for writing this book is for readers to be inspired to see themselves with curiosity and with new possibilities. I want readers to connect to what they already know inside but have not had a way to describe it or to understand it in words, until now. I want readers to come away with tools that make sense to them and enhance their work, life, visions, and dreams. I truly believe that the more we connect to who we are on the inside, the more we shine our true light on the outside, and the happier we are with ourselves. This is where we begin living the life of who we truly are, and the life force within is seen and draws in what we want our life to be.

I named my vision, my business, Express Your Essence®, with the tagline of "Embrace the Power of Your Presence." I believe that when you embrace who you are, your Essence, the magic of your life comes alive. It is as if the door opens to explore who you are. The answer to, "Who am I?" is found when you walk through that door. It is embracing the knowledge of who you are that keeps you moving forward. There are times that we all may get caught up with circumstances and seem to forget and walk blindly again until we find ourselves asking the question, "Who am I?" and that is why I wanted to write this book. I wanted the information to be available at any time and for all time, to be a reminder of how to recognize the true Essence within.

My passion is to help others connect to the beauty of who they are on the inside, how to embrace their unique Essence, and have a way to open the door to love themselves. From this place of self-love, we begin the process of being able to heal and grow from whatever has been holding you back in the past. Understanding your Essence is the yearning that is the reason of the question, "Who am I?"

In this book, I will start the process of helping you to identify your Essence. It is a discovery process; for some it is easy, and for others, it may take some time to find all the nuances of their uniqueness. I am offering you a beginning and perhaps a new way to look at all the ways your unique Essence shows up. I will describe how to support your Essence with the way you are seen in the world and why this supports you in receiving what you desire.

THE DRESS YOUR ESSENCE PROCESS

I have named the process Dress Your Essence, and as I walk you through the steps, I invite you to actively explore, experiment, and have fun! The steps in the process that I will present in this book beginning with The Naked Essence; here I will share the understanding of what "Essence" is and how I interpret the Essence for self-discovery and exploration into how our Essence shows up in all areas of our lives. Then I walk you through how to Discover Your Essence. This is an introduction to explore underneath your self-image. I describe the four Essence Types, so you may begin to see yourself at your inner core. I also take you through a testing process to help you to start identifying your own unique Essence.

Next, you must Undress Your Essence! Here you will begin to see yourself with no outer shell, naked from the personalities that we create to function as a woman, a mother, a wife, a daughter, a sister, an employee, a business owner, and more. Naked of the image created in the past. I will describe the Essence elements of each Essence Type to prepare you to learn how to Dress Your Essence.

After you Undress Your Essence, I will help you identify all the Essence elements in your unique Essence. I will help you develop the words that most describe your Essence in a way that helps you to own it, by creating your own unique Essence Power Statement. You will be able to use this as a reminder of your true Essence on those days when you need a little extra empowerment. With this next step, I will explore how to Dress Your Essence, and I will give you information and tools on how to begin, experiment, and engage with what you choose to wear and why.

I truly wish for you to see and feel what it is like to be aligned with your Essence energy inside and out. If you do the deep work within this book, you will experience that! Magic will happen. You will weave down into the fibers of who you truly are, let go of the exhausting idea of authenticity, and connect with a powerful energy within. The real you will bloom, and you will transform how you present yourself to the world, in life and business.

I invite you to join me on a journey of discovery. Walk away from that place of self-doubt and discomfort, where you try to be authentic, yet no one sees who you really are. Leave behind awkward conversations with prospective clients you know you could serve well, if only they would understand the passion in your heart. You are unique, and your work is important to this world. To support just how special you are, let's forget what you've been taught about the "best" way to present yourself. We'll undress your essence and dress your confidence, embracing your unique style to reveal the real you. Then, you can walk in a room and show who you truly are, without even speaking a word. Thank you for allowing me to guide you through this fun and empowering process.

PART ONE

THE NAKED ESSENCE

"Behold your unique gifts in the context of the energy that defines your true nature, before time begins to dress what it does not understand."

—STEFFI JO

CHAPTER ONE

"DOES THIS LOOK GOOD ON ME?"

"Let the beauty you feel be the path that you follow."

—STEFFI JO

When I think of the most common advice around dressing well, I think of "the little black dress." Women are taught a little black dress is good for every occasion, a closet staple we should all reach for when we don't know what else to wear. I have to smile and giggle because my natural reaction is to throw that little black dress in the shredder! Then, secretly and in my mind, I do a little dance and say, "F#@% that little black dress!" Not because I hate black dresses, but because the little girl in me can't help it but rebel against the idea that one dress type is perfect for every woman in all of our moods and life stages, and for every event. Each time I picture the dress in the shredder, she jumps up and down, all happy and excited to come out and play. She knows that I see her; I recognize her individual spirit; my core Essence and our connection grows stronger. It is an excitement of knowing oneself through the eyes of a curious, innocent child. The adult in me is standing up and saying that I no longer wear the costumes of others to be accepted and fit inside the "box," and I am not here to be like everyone else. I am here to be my most authentic self and follow my own path with the gifts that I have been given. I will no longer wear the costumes of others because they were not made for me. I will learn and understand what works for my Essence and I will be myself outside the "box!" The little girl inside remembers the journey I have walked to get here and is proud of me.

I remember my first day of high school and not feeling like I belonged. I had gone shopping the summer before, and I was excited to find new clothes that I put on layaway, including my most favorite outfit. I loved the textures, the designs, and the colors. I can still feel the soft deep purple velvet bell-bottom pants and the vibrating, colorful zigzag design of the blouse. Walking to school in that outfit made me feel confident and excited. However, the other girls teased me. I only wore that outfit a few more times because I realized I did not fit in with the girls I wanted to be friends with. It led me to believe that if I did not fit in, there must have been something wrong with me. I began asking the same question over and over: Why do I not fit in?

As a young girl trying to figure out how to fit into the outside world, I decided I would look at myself from the outside, as I thought those girls did. I chose to believe it was all about the clothes I wore, and not who I was on the inside. I thought I needed to wear clothes they liked to be accepted. My journey was about how to fit in. In another embarrassing high school moment, I showed up to a dance wearing a striped white and blue dress with puffy sleeves and to my horror realized that everyone else was dressed down in jeans and plaid t-shirts. I spent the entire night hiding in the corner, alone.

I became fascinated with why girls chose certain clothes to wear and how do I choose clothes to fit in, when I am attracted to clothes that are different. I wanted to be accepted and not be an outcast, so I began a life of observing and making choices that did not always feel comfortable on me. I continued feeling awkward and wondered how to change, still looking at life as someone who didn't belong. I am an artist, and at that time, I felt a creative urge to become a fashion designer. As I studied, I felt that, for me, there was a pretense, a funny energy about designing and it was not a career I would pursue. I was missing something; I could not grasp designing clothing without the person who would be wearing the clothes in mind. I was still in high school and decided there must be something else for me, and I moved on. Although, the key, for me, that I came back to years later, was that I was feeling the energy of the clothing.

My studies taught me about the science of energy, physical and metaphysical, and how it applies to who we are as unique individuals. The psychology and energy of our personalities—along with the energy of everything we put around us that supports us or drains us—heals us or hurts us. I especially love to witness and experience the effects of the clothing energy that we put on. It's all about getting down to aligning the energy of who we are inside, with the energy of the clothing we wear on the outside.

When this is achieved, we create our own style, our own unique expression that is inviting and real. I am passionate about understanding just how unique we are and what we look like in visual terms and how that can be used to make choices consciously. This journey brings out the magic in each of us. We are each as special as a snowflake, and we have an individual pattern that can be identified and used to set us apart from the masses. We know our patterns of DNA, of fingerprints, and others, so now it's time to look at what our energy pattern is so that we can relate visually to our environment—and to our clothes.

Imagine if you had a formula that identified your unique element patterns that would help you to create that perfect outfit, that perfect brand, and it helped you take the guesswork out of "Does this look good on me?" and "Is this my color?" You could walk out your door or on stage, on camera, or in a meeting and feel your magic and actually own it! The secret is knowing exactly why you choose the elements (the textures, the design, the colors) you put on and how they support you to be and show your best. This is where I can take you if you are willing to look below the surface and connect with the energy of your Essence. With my help, you will know how to make the choices that truly align with who you are inside.

The little black dress has become an icon for many different reasons. Women embrace it because the fashion industry has created the little black dress as the classic wardrobe staple; women use it for dramatic flair at formal events. It's used as a way for workplaces to avoid drawing attention to their employees, and black clothing is a way to hide the body and look slimmer, taller and minimize imperfections. However, there's a mixed message that is confusing. The little black dress is powerful in some ways and disempowering in others. Black is easy. It's convenient. We've been trained to accept it as the go-to for many different reasons.

Think of a formal event you recently went to; it could be a cocktail party, wedding reception, or an after-hours networking event. Chances are, most of the women at the event were in a black dress. It's accepted and its convenient. Society says it's acceptable, you fit in, therefore, you look good. The Little Black Dress allows women to settle, but I'm here to tell you that you are missing out on an opportunity to understand yourself, get to know your authentic self, and live from a place that radiates your most aligned expression into the world.

Connect with the energy of your Essence and learn what it looks like visually. Create from this knowledge so you may support your life and your business on an authentic level for greater sustainable success. Cultivate your Essence in every way to allow your unique vibrating energy to stand out so the ones that are looking for you can find you: new clients, new friends, or even a special someone. You are here to make a difference in others' lives; you hear that voice inside you that keeps pushing you forward. You are looking for that something that will help you be seen so you may be heard. It is not negotiable to do anything less. You must show up to help others by getting out of the box and become conscious of the energy of your true authentic nature.

No longer hide your Essence. The world wants the real you. Your Essence is powerful beyond measure. Allow it to come out and play in the world. Throw that little black dress in the shredder, perhaps do your own little dance as you step into the elements that support your Essence, and finally feel free from asking, "Does this look good on me?"

CHAPTER TWO

WHAT IS "ESSENCE" ANYWAY?

"Your Essence is your purest, authentic self. It is the sum of your vibrations before you experienced life and created the beliefs that you use to protect that little girl inside."

—STEFFI JO

According to the dictionary, Essence is…

- The permanent as contrasted with the accidental element of being.
- The basic, real, and invariable nature of a thing or its significant individual feature or features.
- The properties or attributes by means of which something can be placed in its proper class or identified as being what it is.
- The intrinsic nature or indispensable quality of something, especially something abstract, that determines its character.

Philosophy, however, has a slightly different definition of Essence. In philosophical terms, Essence is…

- The inward nature, true substance, or constitution of anything, as opposed to what is accidental, phenomenal, illusory, etc.

- The attribute or set of attributes that make an entity or substance what it fundamentally is, and which it has by necessity, and without which it loses its identity.

To understand how to dress your Essence, you must start underneath the layers of the life lived and get down to the naked Essence to truly understand your authenticity. This happens before you know how to choose the clothing that will support your authentic self. (I will talk about Essence interchangeably with energy because your Essence is truly the sum of your vibrations in the purest sense). Since ancient times, man has tried to describe and categorize people as a way to understanding our human nature. Essence is the beginning, it is the beginning of your journey on your path to understanding you and your nature, in the simplest of terms. What better way to start a journey than from the beginning…

ESSENCE AWARENESS

Imagine what you were like when you were born: an innocent ball of love, unique and yet a part of everyone through past generations. Naked of experiences, naked of words, naked of thoughts of this world. You were pure energy born into a miracle of life on earth. You were not defined by anything else except pure love and being. Everything is made of energy and vibrates in a way that is unique to its context in this world. To be aware of your naked Essence is to understand your core, your innocence, your being, your authentic self.

Have you ever been in the presence of someone and felt totally captivated by them? It is their Essence radiating out. Your Essence is the silent presence within you that drives your unspoken words into form and emanates an energy that is seen and felt by others. When you become aware of your naked Essence, embody it, and become confident in your state of awareness, you allow others to know who you truly are inside and out. Now take a moment and see if you can remember a time you felt like something just wasn't working, those around you were just not "getting" you. You were trying to "be authentic" at work or in business, listening to all the advice about putting yourself out there and setting yourself apart from the "competition," and still couldn't get to the next level. Well, this is it. Awareness and understanding your naked Essence is what's missing.

ESSENCE AND AUTHENTICITY

I believe that there has been enough said about being "authentic," and it is time to take the next step to a higher level of authenticity! Imagine what it could mean if your authenticity was ignited, and radiated a presence that was seen and felt by those around you. Could this make a positive impact in your personal life or business? Are you ready for a new conversation? When you connect with your Essence, it takes all the work you have done to be authentic in your life and business to a new, higher level that sets you apart. This new world of visibility speaks! The old ways included the mindset of "fake it till you make it," which was a way to put on a show, as if you knew what you were doing on the outside while you were quickly learning how to do it on the inside! Those days are gone. Today, it is transparency and authenticity that people want. Now that this shift has taken place, it is time for a "new authenticity" to bring about the next level of visibility which will set yourself apart from the mass of authenticity that emerged. Understanding your naked Essence is the beginning of your new authentic self, and of learning how to dress your Essence so your confidence is seen and radiates before you even speak.

We'll explore this concept more in the next chapter but for now, know your Essence is connected to your understanding of how to see your Essence energy in the elements of designs, the colors and textures, that you surround yourself with. Embracing that connection will set your visibility apart so the real you, your Essence, is revealed! Your Essence is the keeper of your confidence. When you learn to connect to your Essence, your confidence cannot hide. The learning process encompasses a process; first comes awareness of your Essence, then understanding it, being it, and finally owning it.

If you've studied psychology, you may have heard of the Four Stages of Competence by Abraham Maslow. I often reference Maslow when

I speak about Essence because the process of learning, understanding, and embodying your Essence is the same as the way humans learn:

- **Stage One**: Unconscious Incompetence
  Not understanding or knowing how to do something.

- **Stage Two**: Conscious Incompetence
  Not understanding or knowing how to do something but recognizing the value in learning a new skill.

- **Stage Three:** Conscious Competence
  Understanding or knowing how to do something, but it requires concentration and focus to complete.

- **Stage Four:** Unconscious Competence
  Completing something effortlessly, as if it's second nature.

THIS IS A JOURNEY

The same stages can be applied to the journey in this book. As you move through the process of discovering your naked Essence, you evolve. From this knowledge you create the best version of you and bring your most authentic presence to everything you do. This, in turn, allows a powerful shift to happen—one where you can change your life.

To understand the meaning of Essence is first to know that we must look through the layers we have created throughout our lives. This is not always an easy task to take on, and there are many ways to accomplish this. Even though there are a lot of psychological meanings that encompass why we build these layers, I will only bring to your awareness that these layers exist. In the last chapter of this book, you'll find resources to help you explore these ideas further, if that draws your interest. But for now, our journey is to find a path that takes us past the layers so we may begin to understand the core energy you were born with. It is this energy that makes up who you are, and how you react, perceive experiences, and make decisions in life.

Your Essence energy also vibrates on the level of your authentic truth. Once you can understand this energy and how to put it into physical and visual terms, you have found the knowledge to support you on the outside. You will have discovered your beingness.

CONNECTING WITH BEINGNESS

Today, I naturally rest in my beingness, but before I began exploring Essence and understanding these ideas, it wasn't a place I was familiar with. Yet I did experience a powerful moment in my beingness, and the memory of that energy has stayed with me over the years.

In those days, I worked full-time in the general aviation industry. My then-husband and I owned and ran a business together which innovated an old aviation process. We were the new kids in the industry and wanted to build relationships, so we attended a conference in New Orleans. It was my first time in the city, and I was thrilled to be there. Around the scheduled itinerary, we had networking lunches and dinners, all business, business, business. My husband fit in easily at these events, but aviation is a masculine business, and I was very visible as the only woman in the room.

Leading up to the conference, I'd been learning to stay connected to my feminine side at work, because that's who I am. I'd practiced staying grounded and present as my true self while in a room full of men. I found the better connected I was to my inner self, the more I was seen and heard with value. I stayed grounded at the lunches and dinners in New Orleans, and the men were wonderfully, professionally attentive. They listened closely to what I said, and I know it's because I had the confidence to come out in my feminine energy, instead of presenting the masculinity they were used to. The more I stayed feminine and confident, the more I was heard and valued for my contribution. I felt acknowledged and accepted for who I was.

After a particularly successful day of meetings, I was feeling my own power for the first time in a long time. I felt whole and complete in myself, without needing anyone else. My husband and I headed out for a dinner date, no work, just relationship. As I sat at the table for two in the center of the steakhouse, embodying my successful day, my power and beingness, I naturally gave my total attention to my husband. I had tunnel vision, focused on nothing but him. The waiters came and went, but I barely saw them, I was so enveloped in him and our conversation. Only one thing crept in: I remember thinking, *That woman on the table next to us is talking about me.* I felt sure of it, and then I heard her tell the waiter, "I'll have whatever she's having!"

I dismissed the moment and returned my attention to my husband. Then, when we stood up to leave, something incredible happened. It was surreal, and I haven't shared it with anyone before putting it in this book because it seemed so odd. But everyone in the restaurant stood up and clapped. I turned red, and the waiter said, "This is for you." He meant the standing ovation wasn't about my husband, because he was the recipient of my focus. It was my total confidence, my beingness, my power that moved the room. Our fellow diners had recognized that I was self-assured, not part of my husband but in relationship with him. Without realizing, I had projected my beingness onto those people, energy came out of me and into the room, and everyone around felt it. It impacted them so much, they felt compelled to stand and applaud.

That is the uncontainable power of connecting with your beingness. You Dress Your Essence in your most authentic way. You understand your individual Essence, you can then identify your unique "Essence edge," and know how to set yourself apart. Then, you attract what you want in your personal and business life, and people are compelled to pay attention. But I didn't get that reaction in the restaurant by just "being authentic." Something much deeper was happening, and that's what we'll explore next.

CHAPTER THREE

BEYOND AUTHENTICITY

"To know my Essence is to claim my freedom, to be who I have come into this world to be!"

—STEFFI JO

I really think there's something in the air these days, a movement happening in this time, pushing every one of us to look deeper within and go beyond authenticity. The message that business owners must "be authentic" has saturated the market so much, and now it feels like the language of yesterday.

Before we were drowned in advice to be authentic, a business was a brick-and-mortar building which was its own being. That's how it was when I started my first business back in the 1980s. Then, the internet became a thing and we moved into an age where the business was the brand, but *we were also the brand*, and we were expected to put our personalities out there. We were told to make people know, like, and trust us as people, as well as a business. Now, everyone is putting their personalities out there in Facebook Lives and Insta Stories, blog posts and videos, and beautifully-designed websites. We've left the information age behind and are working in the attention age, where it's all about visibility and branding ourselves to stand out in a world of almost eight billion people.

In this crowded environment, so many female entrepreneurs find authenticity just isn't working. You try to be your authentic self on your website and in brand photos, on social media, at networking events, and in conversations with others, but you feel like something is missing. It's not energizing; it drains you. Imagine you plan to attend, say, a chamber of commerce meeting, and you know you're supposed to present yourself "authentically." You think about how you'll introduce yourself, what you'll say, and what you'll wear. But you don't yet have the confidence that comes with knowing your Essence, so you pick an outfit you've seen someone else wearing that looks appropriate, or something you've seen in a storefront. You do your hair and makeup, gather a stack of business cards, and head out the door.

But when you get there, you don't feel like yourself. You feel uncomfortable and keep tugging at your skirt or pulling on your blouse sleeves. It's because you dressed the mannequin, not your essence. Perhaps you're being authentic to what a business person like you should look like, but you're not being true to your inner energy, or you're being authentic to who you are—an entrepreneur, a mother, a wife, a creative—but you haven't done the deep work to push past those layers and labels to connect to the innocent little girl inside, who represents who you really are. So you walk around the chamber of commerce meeting room, and no one stops to take notice.

I'm always forward-thinking, assessing and observing what's going on and considering how to improve it. In personality quizzes, I come up as an innovator, a visionary, or some variation of that title. I think, How can we take what's there and make it better. When I noticed everyone seemed tired of the overused word "authentic," and it wasn't even working for many women, I asked, *How can we get past this? How can we be more authentic?*

BEYOND AUTHENTICITY IS PRESENCE

I found myself enveloped in this inescapable feeling that presence was the answer. When you feel like being authentic isn't working, it's because you're lacking presence when you walk into a meeting room, a social media group, or a client conversation. You don't have the presence that magnetically attracts attention and shows who you really are. This is why I'm tired of the conversation about authenticity; it isn't enough on its own. You also have to bring a powerful sense of presence to your work, to your whole being and everything you do, really. Since we're flooded with empty authenticity, we must push beyond it to present ourselves with presence and set ourselves apart in this crowded world.

It takes work to set yourself up so you can walk into a room with undeniable presence. You have to push past all the layers that have stacked up throughout your life and connect to yourself on a higher level of beingness. This is the missing link that will connect us to those we're meant to serve.

That's why this book isn't just about dressing. In fact, you might have already done the dressing thing, learning different systems, discovering if your skin has cool or warm undertones, figuring out your color wheel. But if you want to dress your confidence and show the real you, you have to start with *you*! Beautiful, beautiful you, not the clothes. You must first build a relationship with yourself. It's deep work, but that's what it takes to discover your Essence, build your business, and step-up your life.

There's a lot of talk in the business world about stepping up, leveling up, and higher levels of visibility. There seems to be a pervasive sense that authenticity isn't enough anymore, and different programs are

emerging around putting yourself out there in a different way. As an innovator and visionary, my thoughts are just one step ahead. I'm already there and working on it with my one-on-one clients, and I can see it coming in a bigger way. It's happening. People, especially female entrepreneurs, are asking how to go beyond authenticity, but the conversation is still fuzzy because they don't know how to articulate it. This is the way the world is headed. Presence, which comes through connecting to your Essence, is what it will take.

A lot of this comes down to embracing a growth mindset and knowing in your gut that you must explore and ask questions. This isn't a problem for most entrepreneurs, who usually have a questioning mind, wanting to improve in all areas of life. From what I've seen with my own mentors, I believe if you're not learning and growing, you're dying. You're either going forwards or backwards; there's no staying still. Self-development must be as natural as waking up in the morning. Since you bought this book, I know you want to get to the next level and learn to dress your confidence! You can use your growth mindset, this book, and the right clothes together as a tool to get you there.

Of course, once you step up, it takes practice to keep on growing and moving forwards. Luckily, this is a lot of fun! The practice feels like play, and it creates incredible energy. We play in the dressing room, trying on clothes and picking pieces we love, but dressing is not just dressing. It's so much more. The dressing allows others to know what's going on inside us. It lets us embody our Essence and communicate to the world. The clothes act as a two-sided mirror, reflecting our Essence back into ourselves, so we can carry immense confidence, and also mirroring our inner selves out into the world, so others understand us.

WHY UNDERSTAND YOUR ESSENCE?

When you understand the importance of mirroring out your Essence, you hold incredible power. Think of a person who you have watched walk into a room and command it with their energy. They had presence. They may not even have said anything—but their Essence did. When you understand your Essence, you are able to decide how to influence the world around you. Chances are, you have a piece of clothing, a pair of shoes, or a piece of jewelry that lights you up. When you wear this item, you feel like you have an extra spring in your step. You smile more, are more confident, or more outgoing. People notice your energy and compliment you. Imagine having an entire wardrobe of these items! Can you picture how each day would feel?

Understanding your Essence means you know how to move through your day with a deeper connection to your authentic self. You are confident and aligned with who you really are, without hesitation. This may result in:

- A greater sense of self-awareness;
- A greater sense of happiness and joy;
- Reduced stress and fewer health issues;
- More rewarding social interactions and enhanced relationships;
- The ability to achieve more goals in business and in life; and
- The ability to be a more effective communicator and/or leader.

When you enjoy the freedom that comes with being in your Essence, you will inspire others around you. Life will move with a greater sense of ease and flow because you are synchronized with the natural order

of the universe. You cannot be fully in your Essence and have a bad day—it energetically just isn't possible!

Understanding your Essence means to embrace the power of being in your feminine energy and to know this is your authentic self. To be feminine means to flow, be open to receiving, and move through the world from a heart-centered, nurturing space versus a mind-centered, analytical space. The strength of the feminine Essence can no longer stand on the sidelines and expect to make a difference. How can any of us expect to make a difference by wearing each other's clothing? We are coming of age, and I believe the healing the world is longing for will come with the feminine Essence recognizing her strength that is embodied in her voice. Once you understand your own Essence, you will protect it, and you will find your harmony. Your balance will be felt without the need to compromise it by trying to be someone you are not. When you can own your true Essence, you give others permission to relax into their own authentic energy, as well.

Sometimes women lean too much into their masculine Essence, and it can throw off their internal balance. This began with burning of the bras in the 1960s and reached a height in 1980s, when women believed that to make it in a "man's world," they needed to act like a man—or at least lead with masculine energy. The feminine mindset in the 1980s was to climb the corporate ladder, wear the business power suit with shoulder pads, and pull out the masculine self, which was overall contradictory to the natural balance of a woman's Essence. We had a need to go to that side of the spectrum to fight for women's rights. It was confusing for the feminine Essence during this time of wanting change for women to be heard as equals. It was not sustainable for a woman to maintain holding herself steadfast in her masculine energy when her primary real strength was in her feminine energy. The pendulum will swing, looking for its balance to feel whole again. Eventually, we will find balance as a collective in society.

People are attracted to the confidence, balance, and strength of a woman who embraces her feminine power, her feminine Essence. Remember, it is about knowing yourself and acknowledging that you are exactly who you are meant to be. Once you *own* your Essence, your energy, and your uniqueness, you get to create the life that you desire in abundance!

CHAPTER FOUR

DOES ESSENCE REALLY MATTER?

"Essence is the harmony of vibrations that identifies your uniqueness that has come into this world to express itself."

—STEFFI JO

Your Essence matters because *you* matter! You are your Essence, and there is more significant growth in everything that you set out to accomplish when you understand yourself at a deeper level. You are ever-changing in the outside world, based on what you experience and want to create. Why not learn to grow with the conscious awareness of who you came into this world to become. Walking in alignment from the inside-out drops resistance and opens the door to everything you want to accomplish. When in the flow of alignment, each step allows the attraction of more abundance, more happiness, more success, and more love.

Your Essence as a common denominator of everything you experience and create. By using this to your advantage, you can eliminate outside influences that get in the way of your true nature. The point here is to get down to your core and understand it, so you can use it to consciously create your outside world in alignment with your authentic inside… and ultimately learn to dress your Essence for greater success.

Opportunities will present themselves that didn't before. When you are conscious and present in your Essence, people notice, as they did in that restaurant in New Orleans. When I dress in my Essence, I can be out at the grocery store and have strangers come up to me and say things like, "It's great to see you." There's peacefulness in your day because you aren't wasting time and energy worrying about what you're wearing. Dressing your Essence becomes second nature and allows you to focus on life.

As women entrepreneurs, there is so much we need to focus on. We don't have time to stand in our closet and feel like we have nothing to wear. We don't have the energy to waste wondering if an outfit looks good. Dressing your Essence takes care of this, but it reaches so much further. It seeps into how we brand our businesses, too, because they are an extension of ourselves. It's your Essence that drives you to do what you do, and love what you love. Your Essence propelled you to build your business.

When dressing your Essence is second nature, it shows up in everything you touch, including business. You know which colors to choose for your website and which font looks best on a free download. The design elements that suit your Essence type show up in your branding, because your business is a living, breathing entity in harmony with your inner self. You know what to wear for a video call with a prospective client, when you're presenting on stage, or are attending an important networking event. It's easy to wear "your look" so people—the right people—gravitate to you, wanting to know more. Those decisions come naturally when you operate from your beingness.

You're free, then, to focus on other areas of business; emerging, sharing your message with more people, building, and being successful on a whole new level. You can walk into that networking event and know a big part of your job is already done because everyone there knows who you are without you even having to say a word. They see your heart and the heart of your work. They automatically recognize you as an expert, an influencer, a master of your field. They're ready to listen to whatever you have to say and buy whatever you have to sell.

When I show up in this way, I notice that the other people's authentic selves show up, too! It invites others to engage with me on a higher, more positive level. Visual awareness is vital in attracting people to communicate with you in this way and attracting the right things into your life. Understanding the visuals around you and other people gives you profound insight into the energy you're dealing with. This can be especially helpful when you are developing a personal or business brand and want to attract clients. It can inform you when you consider partnering with another business owner, or joining a coaching program or mastermind, or becoming an affiliate for a product. It can also influence your presence when you go out on a date. We all understand now, based on the research of behavioral sciences, that you have only seven seconds to make a first impression, on a date and in business relationships. Your visual presence will invite the prospective client, business partner, or boyfriend to listen to you, or it will convince them to shut you off.

The next factor is how they feel about your presence. Can they sense that you are confident with yourself? Are you authentic in the way you present yourself or are you "dressing the part?" In other words, are you real or are you wearing a costume?

Reflect on an event or day in your life that you have walked out your door and you felt terrific. Everyone you came in contact with had a positive reaction to you and nothing seemed to go wrong or stand in your way. It was the real you. Think about what you chose to wear that day; was it a hard choice? Or, when you saw the outfit in your closet, did you know, and it was perfect for you? Chances are, it was an easy choice, and this sets you up to walk out the door feeling great inside and out. Your visual presence preceded you. It was your authentic self-loving how you felt, and you projected it in a way that others could really see you.

It is the difference between someone saying to you, "I love that dress you are wearing!" and, "You look great!" When they see you versus the dress you are wearing, they perceive the real you. Your Essence invited them in, and this is an open, warm, and trusting place to be. You were aligned, your outfit is an extension of that inner self. There was no costume, because you were open and honest visually. Opening up your authenticity to the eyes of your clients within the first seven seconds of your initial contact is critical to the success in today's world of setting yourself apart.

We all wear or have worn costumes. It is an unconscious act and, in some circumstances, a conscious choice. It is a choice we make when we look for something to wear that will be accepted by others. The costume is the perception of how to dress for success based on what works for other successful people. There are plenty of books written this subject.

Here's an example: Let's say you are a lawyer working on building your business. You observe another highly successful lawyer, and you decide that you want the same success that she has. As a woman, you notice how she is dressed when she wins cases in the courtroom. You then form a picture in your mind of how successful women lawyers dress, and you work on emulating that same look. You can plug any job, industry, career, business into this scenario and it's the same. When we see a woman who is accomplished, we want to jump in and emulate the same. It is like creating a mannequin of how success looks in our mind and buying that same outfit. It is a big part of why things become trendy. When you wear the same outfit, it becomes a costume. It may feel good, and some parts of it may work for you, but in the end, you do not feel that successful "edge" you were ultimately looking for. You do not "own" the look, because you borrowed it, tried it on, and it is not you. Then you struggle with finding the right look for your business meetings, events, speaking engagements, dates, weddings, etc. As you are shopping, there are times you feel good about what you wear and other times it is just not quite right. There is no real definition as to why. You try another mannequin and another, and you get frustrated. What is missing? You have not yet identified and understand what clothing elements align with the real you, your Essence. When you do, you will know exactly what does not work for you and what is perfect for you. It all starts with you diving in to understand your Essence regarding visual elements and apply those elements to the clothing that you wear.

You must identify the real authentic core of who you are and be able to describe you in visual terms. Too many times I have seen the word "authentic" used in a diluted sense to describe a way to act or be in a situation according to a perceived "right" authentic way for that situation. But is it right for the person's true nature or has she learned the "right" behavior based on perception and social acceptance? Think about the last time you watched someone speak, and they sounded good, but something did not feel congruent in their body language.

You could not put your finger on it, but something did not feel right to you. Your intuition was telling you that something was off. This reaction is when you feel a person is not authentically projecting a presence from their true nature. Their knowledge, words, and thoughts are being heard, and they may have great information, yet you do not feel aligned with them. Their first impression probably was not an authentic one based on their congruency from the inside out, from the core of their Essence. They were wearing the right costume for the event or situation, but they were not wearing the elements that aligned with their Essence.

Here's the difference between authenticity based on a perception of the mind and authenticity based on your core Essence: The communication we have within ourselves that we project to the outside world must come from the sum of all parts of you—your mind, body, spirit—to showcase your authentic self. This is much deeper than relying on just the mind's perception. In this world of information and available resources, to attract the clients that are looking for you, you must set yourself apart from the others. Your internal beacon comes from your Essence, and you are unique, so you must showcase your uniqueness to attract an abundance of clients. An authentic aligned visual presence helps your potential clients see you in a crowd of many.

Dressing your Essence matters when you want to set yourself apart to achieve greater sustainable success. Your Essence matters because it is the energy that fuels you at the very core of your passions. Create a blueprint of your Essence in visual terms and apply it to dressing, branding, home, office, and everything that is an extension of you. You will be seen and heard as an embodiment of your authenticity. Living your passions and making visual choices, so others see the real you is the first step of inviting others to experience what you are here to offer. This book will help you get there!

Your Essence matters because this is the real you and when you are wanting to make a difference, wanting to grow, wanting to inspire, wanting to help others, yourself, your children, your family, your friends, your clients, *you matter*. When you can show others, you matter from the inside out, from your Essence, they will want to matter, too. They will want what you came here to give because it is authentic, it's of your Essence, and it is your gift to offer. Your Essence matters because you matter!

As we grow up, we try on different costumes to find out who we are. Somewhere along the line, we get stuck and only wear one or two of those costumes, thinking that's who we are. For instance, the mother or wife costumes are the most common. We wonder, *Who am I?* and *What happened to me?* Then we go back to experimenting. It is essential to understand that it doesn't have to be one costume or another; you can take parts of them and blend to express your unique style. (For instance, being a mom who dresses with an edge.) How exactly do you figure out your Essence and blend? Let's explore this together in the next chapter.

CHAPTER FIVE

KNOWING YOUR ESSENCE

"If you were a flower, where would you grow?"

—STEFFI JO

When I first started the journey of understanding my Essence and learning how to use it, I was exploring ways to heal my depression. I have always been sensitive and interested in the science that everything is made of energy, so I wondered, *How do I heal myself of this depression by healing my energy? I acknowledge that I am not just my body, I am also my mind and spirit; they are all connected and yet they are separate. By healing one area, I am also affecting all, as a whole. If I heal my body, it helps bring healing to my mind and my spirit.* It made sense! If my body felt right, I was naturally happier in my spirit, and my mind was much more creative and had more positive thoughts. However, it was not enough to work on one area at a time, I was seeking a way to integrate healing *all* areas at the same time. I turned to what was common between all three areas: mind, body, and spirit. It took me back to the science that everything is made of energy. I began to explore healing my energy with energy, and I started with healing with color.

As an artist, I learned in my color theory classes about the research done on the subject of color as a healing tool (chromotherapy) and how color affects the psyche. This fascinated me and made so much sense that I kept digging deeper. I experimented on myself and started surrounding my personal space with colors that aligned with the healing I was searching for. It really got exciting for me when I stood in my closet and looked around at my clothes and decided only to wear those healing colors, as a way to support me even further. It was my understanding that I was affecting my energy at an unseen level and yet my physical body loved the visual presentation of the colors, too. I was transforming my body, my mind, and my spirit at the same time, just by consciously choosing the colors that aligned with the healing that my energy needed at the time. The result was that I started feeling better and I was going about it with conscious effort and control of my choices. But this was only the beginning. There was a deeper level that I wanted to go in understanding my energy, knowing that we are all different.

HEALING WITH SHAPES

Like colors, shapes carry energy you can use to heal the areas of your mind, body, and spirit that need extra care in any given moment. The five main shapes found in clothing designs are listed below, with their healing properties and associations.

- Circle: Promotes healing and awareness; associated with divine connection.
- Triangle: Promotes energy and action; associated with speed.
- Square: Promotes strength and balance, associated with prosperity.
- Hexagon: Promotes peace and calmness; associated with nature.
- Diamond: Promotes pleasure; holds energy the longest and is associated with wealth.

Innately, we go through phases. If we need healing energetically, we are attracted to specific colors and shapes. When I look back, I remember times when I would wear yellow during periods of my life. (Now, I always tell clients that color comes first, but it is important to remember that it is not everything. Color comes first, then other elements come in to support that energy. It all must come together to create your formula, which is explained later in the book.)

CRYING IN MY CLOSET

One day, I found myself hiding in my walk-in closet. My whole family was facing a difficult situation and was going downhill because of the trauma that was happening. I was at a loss. I knew I had to be strong for my family because they couldn't be. I had to pull my strength to help my family. *What could I do to help?* I knew there was healing that had to come from within. My intuition told me to look at the energetic aspects.

My closet was where I would go to cry, and that day I asked the universe for help. *What can I do for me so that I can be strong and help others?* In a color training, I had taken previously, I learned about wearing color for healing. We gravitate toward colors for specific healing purposes. So, I started that day and put on the color I was drawn to, yellow. Over time, I added more healing colors to my wardrobe. I felt a shift and believed in it. Even though I was overweight at the time, the changes in my closet were making a difference in the way I showed up in my environment.

I wondered, *How do I put this all together? Is there a system out there that blends the healing of color and the psychology of color in fashion?* After some research, I realized that nobody was connecting it all together in this unique way. The little black dress, among other ideas, remained the standard "box" for women. If we are all different, how can we be put into the same boxes? How can we all be told to wear a little black dress? As I became more in tune with the colors that I felt good in, I would feel an uncomfortable difference when I would try on a black dress. I tried dressing by other color systems, but I still felt uncomfortable and constricted. I knew there had to be something that supports us in integrating colors and designs while allowing us to thrive as unique individuals. If that did not exist, then I would create it!

Getting to know the energy of who I am as a whole person became an intimate process. I soon realized that my unique Essence is under my layers, at my core, where all my energy and life begins. To know my Essence is a way to claim my freedom to be who I came into this world to be.

GETTING TO KNOW YOUR ESSENCE

What is the process of getting to know your Essence? It's about dissecting your "knowingness" of your innate knowledge of yourself. Your Essence gives you hints about who you are at your core when you are by yourself. To get a better idea of your Essence, pay attention to yourself when you are alone, whether at home or in public, and feeling happy. (When people are alone and in a depressed or desperate moment, they grasp for anything external to help them "get out the door" and function as a person. It hides their true Essence.) Notice when that positive feeling is present, the one that you embrace with a feeling of peace within. This is when you feel most complete and whole. Look around and notice the details of where you are; what words come to mind? How would you describe the moment? What colors are present? Your Essence is making its presence known. I want to help you connect to and understand how beautiful and unique you are. Your Essence is waiting for you to discover it. It will support you in "getting out the door," even when you don't feel like it. The smallest thing, like the right color, can lift your mood and brighten your day. Once you understand your Essence, your world opens up.

IF YOU WERE A FLOWER

"If you were a flower, where would you grow?" I ask my clients. I propose this question to everyone seeking to understand their Essence, because it allows the mind to explore from the outside looking within. Now, I want to invite you to imagine where you would grow if you were a flower. Really daydream about this and see the detail in your mind's eye. To know your Essence is to listen to what you see as you explore this idea.

- Are you in a garden, a meadow, or somewhere else entirely?
- What do you see?
- Where have you planted your roots?
- Do your roots reach deep or skim the surface?
- What smells surround you?
- What do your leaves feel?
- Are you soaking up the sunshine or the rain?

I loved doing this exercise, letting my imagination flow freely as I visualized my flower's surroundings, and invited all my senses to join my inner self in this exploration. The environment your flower grows in may be very different from mine, but I want to share my answer to inspire and encourage you to push deep into your daydream. There are no right or wrong ways to explore this question, but here is my example:

"I would grow on a lush desert mountain, where I can see the earth and all its great formations. The desert in which I grow is abundant and full of life. The Saguaro cactuses are tall and noble; the desert flowers in the spring are colorful, exotic, and beautiful. Yet, they are not flowers that you pick to put in a vase to display. These flowers are free and flourish in an untamed environment. The smells are earthy and rich, especially after the rain. The boulder formations are ancient and have stories to tell about a time long ago. It is a colorful desert and full of textures that can be felt with the eyes. The dry washes, where water once flowed and stays beneath the ground, can be followed to hidden pools of water that will cool you in the afternoon sun. The stars at night twinkle like magic tickling the imagination. The animals that scurry around me have purpose and intentions, a sense of survival keeps them thriving.

"I come alive in the spring when new growth is peeking out from the colder nights of the year. The seasons are mild on my desert mountain. It is a place that I watch life from, and I feel connected to it as my roots grow and the wind flutters my leaves. I imagine myself flying with the hawks along the mountain ridges. I feel the strength and determination of this land in which I am planted; it holds me steady and firm as I stretch my petals to gather the sun's rays. I am connected to the earth, and I am lifted by the sky above me. I encompass and absorb all that I am and all that surrounds me. This is where I feel at peace, this is where I come alive, this is where I grow."

—STEFFI JO

Describing where you would grow as a flower comes from your knowingness of that safe, precious place that you love to be when you are all alone. It is your place of not depending on anyone but yourself to be content and fulfilled. It is your "happy place."

Now, it's your turn! Take some time to answer this question and get descriptive with what you see around you. The more you can dive into the details of where you grow, the more you will begin to understand what makes up the energy of your Essence. The environment you grow in is linked to your core energy.

ESSENCE TYPES AND THEIR FLOWERS

Soon, we will explore the four Essence types. We'll use your response to the flower exercise and your answers to the upcoming quiz to connect to your Essence type: one, two, three, or four. For now, here's how different Essence types might answer the flower question. Is there one or more that you strongly relate to?

- Essence Type 1 – Potted plant
  On a quiet windowsill or terrace in a chic city; New York or Paris, would be perfect!

- Essence Type 2 – Meadow
  Where you can feel the breeze flow softly across your leaves as the sun caresses your petals, swaying to the music!

- Essence Type 3 – Rugged terrain
  Feeling at home among the strength of mountains or a cliff overlooking the sea, determined to grow!

- Essence Type 4 – Poppy fields
  Or perhaps amidst wildflowers, the more abundance of flowery friends, the more to dance with!

Where you would grow as a flower can help you to identify your energy and how to use your information when dressing and other areas of your life. Keep note of which type(s) you identified with and let's discover which Essence Type you really are.

PART TWO

UNDRESSING YOUR ESSENCE

"The most intimate of all the journeys we take during our lifetime is the journey within. This journey has no limits to which you may travel. The paths are many. The choices are yours."

—STEFFI JO

CHAPTER SIX

THE ESSENCE DISCOVERY PROCESS

"'Proceed with caution,' says the Ego.

'Proceed with excitement,' says the Heart.

'Proceed with knowing the familiar path of coming home,' says the Soul."

—STEFFI JO

Discovering your Essence is about awakening your innate knowledge of who you are deep down inside at your very core—without all the layers you have created from your life experiences. It is not enough to speak your truth; you must show your truth. In this way, you are consistently congruent, and you have the edge of true authenticity that genuinely attracts others. You create your very own personal Law of Attraction energy around you.

How do you get there? How do you break through the layers? How do you know that you have made it through the layers of personality you have created to fit your lifestyle and the environment you have lived within? We all wear costumes and build personalities based on our Essence. It is an unconscious choice based on our experiences, and sometimes it is a conscious choice to be and act a certain way to fit in or to get what we want. We may have more than one costume, personality, or identity, such as parent, child, employee, entrepreneur, spouse, and others. This is how we function in the life we create, but do you feel congruent with them all or do you feel disconnected? When there is a disconnection, we are basing our identities and behaviors on beliefs that we created because of experiences, and we put a barrier over our authentic Essence. We make choices to fit in and to be accepted by others. We make decisions that create a picture of how a loving parent should speak, or how a successful entrepreneur should dress, or how a model employee should behave. They are all choices based on our beliefs.

Discovering your Essence, beyond the barriers that lie beneath the identities and behaviors that you have created through the years, is the key to building an authentic, congruent you from the inside out. Building a congruent, authentic visual presence is at the core of all successful personal brands. It shows up in everything you do, and your presence becomes something that cannot be ignored. You are noticed and perceived as someone who "walks their talk," and others feel your energy before you even speak.

The first step I will take you through is a simple Essence typing process. The process that I have created is pulled from all the most popular personality tests. From my research, I have found that they all come from the same philosophy that originated from Socrates to Hippocrates a few thousand years ago. They were further developed through the ages by Plato, Galen, Pavlov, Adler, Fromm, Jung, and Keirsey, among many more. All the personality typologies are fundamentally in alignment with each other. Some philosophers go deeper into developing certain aspects of the personalities to create a broader and more detailed exploration of the types, and they all can be funneled to a description of basically four categories. I correlate and focus on the energy of the four personality types and the systems that highlight the energy levels of the types. I also pull from the scientific knowledge that everything is made from energy and the understanding of how the energy flows and supports each type at their very core, their Essence. I get very excited when I explore the energy of people, places, and things. I really connect to the science of energy that makes up everything! I get even more excited when I explore who I am and what I am made of in mind, body, and spirit. I believe that considering just one of these without the other does not give us the whole picture of who we are on a conscious, authentic level.

I want to be very clear and transparent as you go through the process of discovering and recognizing your true Essence. I have no new information to give to you that has not already been put out into this world through the ages or in recent years. I have no new details on dressing in the latest fashion or styles. I am not a fashion consultant or designer. Instead, I am a woman who has struggled, beginning as a young teenager, with choosing between clothes that made me feel good, and clothes to help me "fit in" and be accepted by others. Often, I chose to fit in and be accepted despite who I really was on the inside. I chose to mask the real me, unconsciously believing that to be accepted and successful I must dress my belief of what that was, even though I felt awkward. For example, having a belief of what a "popular girl" dressed like would influence what I'd wear, even though those choices did not "fit" me and I wouldn't receive the same positive results. Everything felt off. You already have an innate sense of what you love to wear, what colors and what textures make you feel good. Now, it's time to trust that. I've taken all my learning, knowledge and research over the last forty years to focus on helping women feel good about who they are and align their outside with their innermost Essence.

On this discovery Path, I will give you an Essence typing journal exercise that will help you become clear on your unique Essence traits. This exercise is important because it will allow you to drop the many hats you wear during the day, and will free your mind to answer

ESSENCE TYPING JOURNAL EXERCISE

Step 1. Remember Feeling Aligned

Take out a piece of paper and pen. Go back and remember a moment in your past where everything seemed to be aligned. This could be prom, your wedding day, a first date, or any time you felt in your true being.

- How did you feel?
- What were you wearing?
- Was the material shiny, dull, smooth, or rough?
- Were there buttons or zippers?
- What colors were you wearing?
- What did you love about yourself at that time?
- What did you see?
- What did you hear?
- What was going on around you?
- What compliments did you get?

instinctively. There are no right or wrong answers. The goal is to be free of opinions or judgments about who you are now versus who you were before, when you were innocent and free of the experiences that have shaped your roles today. For some, this will be a natural process. For others, getting past the roles they have created will be confusing.

As we go through the process, my desire is to help you find your true Essence, and I will keep expanding the Essence Types in ways that will help you identify what may have seemed unclear in the beginning. Trust the process and I will guide you to dress your Essence with purpose, clarity, fun, and successful results. I ask that you allow yourself the freedom to come and play with me on this journey! You already have an innate sense of your Essence, and I'll help you look even closer.

In the Essence typing journal exercise below, you'll be prompted to write about experiences in your past and how they made you feel. Set aside some quiet time when you can explore these thoughts and write freely about them, knowing you are safe, and no one will see your words. This doesn't need to be "perfect," just honest. The specific questions will guide you through this journaling exercise, but you are welcome to write more if you feel called to. Enjoy this opportunity to connect to moments in your past, even if it's uncomfortable, as the deeper understanding you gain will give you powerful insights into your Essence Type.

HEALING WITH COLOR

Before we delve into that deeper level, let's explore how those colors in my closet energized my healing, with a short list of colors and their healing energies. When you understand the power of a pure color, you can use it to heal your mind, body, and spirit. Then, in future chapters, we'll discover the effects of the various shades, tints, and hues of each color. Use this list as a first step to choosing healing colors for whatever is troubling you.

- Red: Brings warmth, energy, and stimulation; promotes love, sex, and courage.
- Orange: Is warm, cheerful, liberating; promotes health, creativity, and self-expression.
- Yellow: Helps with nerves, awakens the mind, and revitalizes life.
- Green: Brings balance and harmony; soothes the body and promotes healing.
- Blue: Alleviates inflammation; brings cool and calm energy.
- Purple: Promotes transformation and detoxification; increases spiritual connection.
- White: Considered the "perfect color" because it is all colors combined; raises vibrations and promotes spiritual peace.
- Pink: Heals grief and sadness; promotes emotional healing, love, femininity; restores youthful energy.

- Brown: Stabilizes and grounds energy; improves focus and decision-making.
- Gray: Neutralizes negative energy; is reserved and refined.
- Black: Protects energy; wards off negativity and opens up deep awareness. Also associated with luxury, elegance, and sophistication.
- Gold: Promotes good luck, abundance, and creativity; associated with authority, power, and luxury.
- Silver: Promotes intuition; associated with healing, rebirth, and psychic abilities.

Step 2. Remember The Opposite

Journal about a specific moment when you felt at your worst, such as a school dance.

- How did you feel?
- What were you wearing?
- Was the material shiny, dull, smooth, or rough?
- Were there buttons or zippers?
- What colors were you wearing?
- What did you love about yourself at that time?
- What did you see?
- What did you hear?
- What was going on around you?
- Did you receive any negative comments?

Step 3. Compare These Two Memories

Write down any contrasts you notice between the two memories. Notice colors, textures, clothing details, and so on. These insights are the beginning of understanding your Essence. They will give you something to relate to when you look at the results of the Essence typing quiz in the next chapter.

CHAPTER SEVEN

THE ESSENCE TYPING QUIZ

"Remembering the truth of who you are is the real test of living a full and happy life."

—STEFFI JO

How do you get to the truth of who you are? How do you understand you and how you relate to energy and design elements? Once you learn this, you will approach your closet and department store in a new, exciting way! I am going to give you a perspective in visual terms—a new understanding of how to see the energy of design elements and how they align with your own energy.

The more successful you become in understanding your own unique Essence Type and the design elements that match your Essence energy, the more aligned you become inside out. This is when the magic happens! Let's begin.

INTRODUCING THE ESSENCE TYPING QUIZ

Soon, you will take an Essence typing quiz that will help you develop an understanding of the four Essence Types. The initial breakdown of the Essence is about your basic formula or percentage of all the types. You have all the Essence Types within you; it is a matter of understanding the percentages of each, how they affect your energy, and how to use your formula in the way you dress.

I bet that most of you have done personality typing processes in the past, and this is similar. The fact is they are all the same with a few variances. This is because there is no new information on this planet! The human typing systems can be traced back approximately two thousand five hundred years, to Hippocrates/Galen's typing of the Four Temperaments of Human Nature: Sanguine, Melancholy, Choleric, and Phlegmatic. It is fascinating how they were considering the body and the personality when diagnosing someone and deciding how to put them back in balance. The Essence Types differ from these other systems because they expand on how the energy of the body, the mind and personality, and the spirit must all be considered when dressing in alignment to bring about wholeness and balance.

In my quiz, I have chosen words to bring out the energy of the personality, so we may begin to understand yours, and correlate it to the energy of your clothes. Remember, science has taught us that everything is made of energy. It is a basic fact. The rate of the energy's vibration is important, though. What is your vibration and that of the clothing that you wear and how do they work together?

Below is a comparison of some of the more popular personality tests—ones that you may be familiar with. These tests are usually given for reasons of classification, for group and teams, for strengths and weakness in job positions, along with many others. When you take these tests, you usually put your mind into a thought process to answer them from how you react to others in these situations. I am going to ask you to think differently before you take the Essence typing quiz. You do not want a result based on what or how you think as your mom-self, work-self, parent-self, spouse-self, your business-self, friend-self, or any other position or role you are responsible for in life. I am talking about you at your core with no outside distractions!

THE FOUR PERSONALITY TYPE EQUIVALENTS

The list below shows personality typing systems and how they are in alignment with each other, with the differences being in names, usage, industries, and more. You will see the Essence Types in this comparison, too. The basic types are the same. There are no new basic personality discoveries, just new understandings of the degrees, and how they apply to you. We will start here with the basic classification before we move on to the energy of the Essence Types and the Essence typing quiz.

Hippocrates' Greek Terms (370 BC): Phlegmatic, Melancholy, Choleric, Sanguine.

Plato (340 BC): Philosopher, Scientist, Guardian, Artisan.

Western Astrology: Water, Earth, Fire, Air.

Enneagram: Peacemaker, Asserter, Adventurer, Helper.

(Enneagram): Observer, Perfectionist, Achiever, Romantic.

Sprangler (1930): Theoretic, Economic, Religious, Aesthetic.

Fromm (1947): Receptive, Marketing, Hoarding, Exploiting.

Merrill-Reid: Amiable, Analytical, Driver, Expressive.

D.E.S.A.: Solid, Analytical, Dominant, Expressive.

DiSC: Influence, Cautious Compliance, Dominance, Steadiness.

The P's: Peaceful, Perfect, Powerful, Popular.

The S's: Solid, Systematic, Self-Propelled, Spirited.

The A's: Amiable, Analytical, Administrative, Active.

LEAD Test: Dependable, Analyst, Leader, Expressor.

"What's My Style?" (WMS): Considerate, Systematic, Direct, Spirited.

McCarthy/4MAT System: Innovative, Analytic, Common Sense, Dynamic.

PSI: Supporter, Analyst, Controller, Promoter.

Animals: Dolphin, Owl, Bear, Monkey.

Comics: Cathy, Ziggy, Jason, Snoopy.

Who Moved My Cheese? by Spencer Johnson, M.D.: Haw, Hem, Sniff, Scurry.

David W. Keirsey: Guardians: SJ, Idealists: NF, Rationals: NT, Artisans: SP.

The 4 Gospels: St. Mark, St. John, St. Matthew, St. Luke.

The Color Code by Dr. Taylor Hartman: White, Blue, Red, Yellow.

True Colors® (1978): Blue, Gold, Green, Orange.

Children's Literature: Pooh, Eeyore, Rabbit, Tigger.

Charlie Brown Characters: Charlie Brown, Linus, Lucy, Snoopy.

Essence Types: Essence Type 1, Essence Type 2, Essence Type 3, Essence Type 4.

Now that you can see how the personality typing systems line up, you could say that you have a pretty good idea what your Essence Type might be. This is a good beginning. However, to understand your Essence Type and how to dress it on the outside, you need to understand the energy of your Type and what roles the other Essence Types play in your unique Essence Formula. The Essence Types are on the list for a general comparison to the others. I am going to expand this knowledge to include the energy of your Type and include how your mind, body, and spirit play a role when it comes to Dressing Your Essence.

THE ESSENCE TYPING QUIZ & INSTRUCTIONS

This quiz will help you awaken the awareness that you know who you are, so you can see which Essence Type is strongest within you. Psychologists, psychiatrists, philosophers, and anyone in the human development field have used these tests for many reasons in their work, to be able to understand people and how they react, accept and think about themselves and their environments. Since Hippocrates, the father of western medicine, and then Plato, who helped to lay the foundation of western philosophy, scientists and philosophers have studied how people basically function from a dominant personality type. They all have put their own work and research into understanding how people do what they do, and they all align with the same basic four personality types. They have not changed for two thousand five hundred years and are the foundation for all personality tests today.

Your Essence typing quiz is based on all the same information as all other personality tests, as there is no new information after two thousand five hundred years! However, I use this information to identify your most core, authentic, pure personality, your Essence, the one that you came into this world with, not the one you created from your experiences or to be in your chosen environment. Then, I'll reveal how your Essence Type shows up naturally in your responses to the physical environment you create, in what you choose to surround yourself with, and in what you choose to wear.

Dressing your Essence captures the personality types into the philosophy that we are all artist of our lives and we are the art! As a painter uses every stroke to create a certain pattern and texture upon the canvas, in conjunction with the light of color in different hues and shades to create an energy of movement, that evokes the viewer to feel or to perceive the true meaning of the painting, I teach how to understand your own personality palette and design elements to enhance the way you want to feel when choosing what to wear.

By understanding how to dress your Essence you take the guesswork out of the process when shopping for just the right outfit, when it matters to you what you project to your audience, your clients, your meetings, your social events, etc. This awareness is not about fashion or style; it is about being able to choose the elements within a style that aligns with your authentic self. The effect of dressing with your Essence in mind creates an internal feeling of positive confidence and an external projection that you are authentic. What does it look like when you observe someone who is "walking his or her talk"? Can you sense this before they speak? If they are congruent inside and out, you can see it! Are there situations or events that you wish not to waste time and know what to wear? Would you like to have a closet full of clothes that all enhance your Essence authentically, without guesswork? If so, learn about your Essence and how to dress it!

Below is a simple quiz to discover your primary Essence Type. Check the words below that your friends would describe you as when you were growing up, at a time when you had no cares or worries, at a time when you remember being happy as a child. This is not a personality test to determine who you are at work, as a mom, or any other role you play in your everyday life. This is a quiz to determine how you are made up on the inside, your most authentic self! So, let go of any labels, just be you, and choose the words that best describe the person inside that you feel and others see!

Please note that you have within you all of the types and will most likely select words from all of them. That is okay; the intention is to find the Essence Type with whose words you resonate the most. Thus, you can know your primary Essence Type for the purpose of dressing your Essence!

THE ESSENCE TYPING QUIZ

For each question, check the one word that best describes you when you were young, playing on the playground with your friends. If you can't decide on just one word, you can choose two. Then, you'll add up your scores for a, b, c, and d answers, and you will have the beginnings of your Essence Formula.

1. a) articulate, b) accurate, c) adventurous, d) animated.

2. a) pleasant, b) perfectionist, c) productive, d) playful.

3. a) skeptical, b) subtle, c) strong-willed, d) spontaneous.

4. a) contemplative, b) conscientious, c) competitive, d) curious.

5. a) responsible, b) romantic, c) rational, d) refreshing.

6. a) stable, b) supportive, c) self-reliant, d) social.

7. a) peaceful, b) patient, c) pioneer, d) promoter.

8. a) smooth, b) sweet, c) stimulating, d) sincere.

9. a) orderly, b) observer, c) outspoken, d) optimistic.

10. a) firm, b) factual, c) forceful, d) fresh.

11. a) disciplined, b) delicate, c) daring, d) delightful.

12. a) cultured, b) consistent, c) confident, d) cheerful.

13. a) idealistic, b) innocent, c) impatient, d) inspiring.

14. a) diplomatic, b) dependable, c) decisive, d) demonstrative.

15. a) mediates, b) moody, c) motivates, d) merry.

16. a) tactful, b) tolerant, c) tenacious, d) talkative.

17. a) loyal, b) listener, c) leader, d) lively.

18. a) consistent, b) contented, c) controller, d) charming.

19. a) poised, b) permissive, c) productive, d) popular.

20. a) basic, b) balanced, c) bold, d) bouncy.

21. a) bland, b) blended, c) bossy, d) bright.

22. a) unbending, b) unenthusiastic, c) unsympathetic, d) uncontrolled.

23. a) resentful, b) reluctant, c) resistant, d) repetitious.

24. a) fixed, b) fussy, c) frank, d) fickle.

25. a) insecure, b) indecisive, c) impatient, d) interrupts.

26. a) unreceptive, b) uninvolved, c) unaffectionate, d) unpredictable.

27. a) finicky, b) fluctuates, c) fiery, d) fanciful.

28. a) cool, b) clean, c) certain, d) cute.

29. a) authoritative, b) aimless, c) ambitious, d) agile.

30. a) neutralizing, b) nonchalant, c) nervy, d) naïve.

31. a) seclusive, b) sourpuss, c) steadfast, d) sureness.

32. a) temperamental, b) timid, c) tactless, d) twinkle toes.

33. a) devoted, b) doubtful, c) domineering, d) dramatic.

34. a) idealistic, b) indifferent, c) intolerant, d) innocent.

35. a) majestic, b) mumbles, c) manipulative, d) messy.

36. a) skeptical, b) sympathetic, c) stubborn, d) show-off.

37. a) loner, b) lazy, c) leader, d) loud.

38. a) suspicious, b) shy, c) short-temper, d) silly.

39. a) rigid, b) reluctant, c) rash, d) restless.

40. a) critical, b) compromising, c) conclusive, d) colorful.

Now add up the number of a, b, c, and d answers you circled above, and enter the totals below.

Total a's:

Total b's:

Total c's:

Total d's:

If you have mostly a's, you are primarily Essence Type 1.

If you have mostly b's, you are primarily Essence Type 2.

If you have mostly c's, you are primarily Essence Type 3.

If you have mostly d's, you are primarily Essence Type 4.

WHAT DOES YOUR ESSENCE TYPE MEAN?

Now that you have finished the initial Essence typing quiz, I can talk to you more specifically about the Essence Types and how *you* relate to them. I will describe each type further in the coming chapters, but for now, it is important for you to remember that you have all types within you. The results we are aiming for in the testing process is the Essence Type you naturally reside in; your "go-to" instinct and which ones support you the most in order of secondary strength and so on. The purpose of the Essence Typing quiz is to find your formula—the balance of your primary type with your secondary, and so on. Then, as you continue to learn and grow in this process, you will go through a "fine-tuning" and adjust your formula. For now, read about each Essence Type and pay attention to the results from your answers.

As you learn about each element that aligns with your Essence Type, ask yourself, "Did I answer from my mind, my heart, or my spirit?" If you answered from your mind's point of view, it most likely means you have a picture in your mind of someone you know who is successful, and you want to emulate what they wear. If you answered from your heart's point of view, it is most likely because you are triggered by an emotion you are looking to have fulfilled. If you answered from your spirit's point of view, it is most likely your innate intuition pushing you from your energy of knowingness; you can't help it, sometimes you just know.

TRUST AND EXPERIMENT

I ask that you trust the process. It takes experimenting with the elements of your type to find your magic formula. You will know it when you feel it, when you see it, and when you experience it. Allow the process to unfold as I take you further down this path, and you will arrive at the gate to your unique Essence. Walking through the gate is your choice.

Go back to your journaling from the last chapter with the results of your Essence typing quiz and see how it relates to your best and worst memories. Did your memories match up with your primary or secondary Essence Type? Did your best memory match up with your primary? If not, where are you not feeling confident? Also, reflect on the flower exercise from chapter five. The type of flower you most identified with is a reflection of your primary Essence Type.

I want to share an example from Mary. Mary was drained. She felt dull, unhappy, and bored, as though she were "stuck" in life. She took the Essence typing quiz, which revealed her primary Essence Type is 2, and her secondary is Type 4. Without being aware of it, she had been making clothing choices mostly of Type 3, and they were very draining on her. She had shied away from choices that align with her primary Essence Type 2. When she went to the mall, she would choose Type 3 clothes, because she believed that was best for her. She never quite felt on top of her game wearing clothes with Type 3 design elements because she is Type 2.

After learning the results of her quiz, Mary experimented dressing in the colors and design elements of Type 2 and added some elements of her secondary Essence Type 4. Mary paid close attention to how she felt and noticed a difference. She was confident and energized as she headed out to work each morning. Slowly, she started replacing her wardrobe with outfits aligned to her Essence Type 2/4.

Mary had acknowledged the Essence Type that was draining her, redirected her energy to align with her true, primary Essence Type, and supported her efforts with elements from her secondary Type. She felt more centered in her Essence and was able to navigate her days with renewed excitement! Now you know your Essence Type, let's discuss what that means, and how to align with your primary and secondary Types for more excitement in your own life.

CHAPTER EIGHT

SO... WHAT DOES YOUR ESSENCE TYPE LOOK LIKE?

"Essence is the core of all things; therefore, you are all things."

—STEFFI JO

You have all the Essence Types within you. The question is this: What does your primary Essence Type mean, and in what order does your Essence rely on its strengths? From the Essence typing quiz in the last chapter, you were given words to choose from that represented some of the strengths from each type. Then, your results produced your strongest to your weakest Essence Formula. I will provide you with descriptions of each Essence Type to digest and, as you read them, see if your Essence Formula—that balance of your primary Type with the other three—matches the way you feel towards each Essence Type description. This is just the beginning of a fun exploration of the energy of the elements each Essence Type is aligned with and feels the most alive within.

I describe each Essence Type in terms of design elements that can be applied to the clothing choices you make. They are also elements that you will find that you naturally surround yourself with. We will explore the unconscious reason why. It is your natural personal Law of Attraction, and you will find you already have your Essence design elements in your closet—they may already be your favorite clothes to wear! You will also see that you have clothing in your closet that you don't wear because they do not include enough of your Essence Type design elements to help you feel your best.

When you understand and apply your new knowledge, it is like a new light bulb making your closet brighter. Now you can make conscious choices that align with your core Essence inside-out. Imagine how much easier shopping will be when you know what design elements are best for you!

As you read the following descriptions of each type, you will be able to confirm which Essence is "mostly" you and as we continue the process in later chapters, we will check the other Types and define the elements that are also essential for your wardrobe. One more thing: I want you to understand that these are design elements that can be applied to any fashion or style you are attracted to wear. It is a matter of choosing the clothing piece within your style or fashion preference that includes the design elements that represent your Essence.

ESSENCE FASHION AND STYLE VERSUS ESSENCE ELEMENTS

Understanding the difference between your fashion or style choice and your Essence elements is key to developing your authentic visual presence. In the process of dressing your Essence, whichever fashion and style you choose to live within is the first choice you make. The second choice is to always select the design elements of your Essence formula. I call these "Essence design elements." They are incorporated into the way the clothing piece is made, thus creating alignment with your authentic energy. Your fashion or style preference represents your personality that you have created on the outside as a connection to the world you want to live within. When your Essence elements are incorporated into your fashion or style, they present your authentic connection from the inside-out. This gives you edge in your personal or business branding, when you want to look and feel exceptional for all occasions, or just walking out your door to the grocery store!

Fashions change season to season, year to year, but your Essence remains constant. You can apply your Essence elements to any style, so no matter what is popular these days, you can always find something in the mall that you will love, that is in alignment with your inner child. So if the fashion is long skirts, you can apply your Essence Formula and choose a long skirt that has a A Line, or is straight, or has a small, busy pattern, or a bold, block of color. The same is true for those "rules" about body type: the pear, apple, hourglass, or rectangle categories most women's bodies are supposed to fall into. Your Essence Type elements can be applied to any guidelines you want to follow about dressing for your shape. These guidelines, though, should always come after Dressing Your Essence. It's so easy to get stuck on choosing the right clothes for your shape, or your colors, or the latest fashion, but if you start with your Essence, everything else will fall into place. Your inner child will actually enjoy playing with this season's most popular colors, because your Essence Type will guide you in adapting those colors to align with your Essence.

THE ESSENCE TYPES EXPLAINED

The following are the Essence Types and their energy elements in general terms to give you an initial sense of each Type and to help you further identify with your Essence. You already innately know which type you are but may not be entirely confident in which is your core primary Essence Type.

ESSENCE TYPE 1

Essence Type 1 is the calmest of all the Essence Types. People with this type vibrate with subtle, quiet strength and little movement. They are noticed for their steady consistency in life.

- Example: actress *Audrey Hepburn.*

Essence Design Elements

- Little or no designs in clothing pattern and little or no movement in fabric choices reflect the calm inner energy of this type.

- The quieter the design and the less movement in the fabric, the more it is aligned with their Essence and the clearer their statement is made.

Design Patterns

- No pattern: The most calming design element is no pattern. That is very appealing to this Essence Type.

- Straight line(s): A little energy movement; the fewer lines, the better. An artist can paint one long and bold stroke of color on a blank canvas and create a stunning statement, which is an example of this Essence Type.

- Long and sleek shapes: A little energy movement in design shapes, such as elongated ovals or rectangles. The long, sleek design has a slow, graceful movement quality.

- Large and bold shapes: The larger a design shape, the less energy is reflected outward. The bolder the shape, the less energy is expended, and less is needed. These shapes hold the strength of this type within and allow others to experience them without words.

- Symmetrical and balanced: This also creates a quiet energy full of strength.

Fabric Characteristics

- Smooth, slick, and clean: These texture elements reflect the most calming fabric choices for this Essence Type.

- Very structured: The more structure to fabric, the less energy movement. Structured terms: firm, sleek, stiff, simple, and bold.

Color

- Pure color (hues): The calmest and still colors that reflect the bold, peaceful and quiet strength of Essence Type 1 are pure colors. These colors on the artist palette and color wheel are the hues. Hues are fully saturated colors.

- White: The energy of pure white aligns with Essence Type 1 for two reasons: One, in the visible sense, white is defined as the reflection of all hues, and two, in the pigment sense, white is defined as the absence of all hues.

- Black: The energy of pure black aligns with Essence Type 1 for two reasons: One, in the visible sense, black is defined as the complete absorption of all hues, and two, in the pigment sense, black is defined as the presence of all hues.

ESSENCE TYPE 2

Essence Type 2 is the next in motion, the energy going from calm to flowing waves vibrating with caressing strength and picking up movement. People with this Essence Type are noticed for their nurturing, compassion and attention to detail in life.

- Example: actresses *Marilyn Monroe* and *Mila Kunis.*

Essence Design Elements

- With the energy of flowing waves the design elements are introduced, slowly staying with little or low to medium design patterns in fabric choices. The little to medium movement gives intention and purpose for this type to move forward in alignment with their Essence.

- The movement of Essence Type 2 designs becomes more open and clearer with every step taken.

Design Patterns

- Limited or sparse pattern: A flowing pattern leaving open spaces. Too much pattern would create too much energy for this Essence Type.

- Curved or wavy lines: Moving with the flow creates curved lines or wavy lines, especially in a downward direction.

- Teardrop and soft shapes: The energy of a teardrop design shape represents a soft movement. This Essence Type connects with soft S shapes and curves. This type aligns mostly with soft corners.

- Blended patterns: Blended patterns have a flowing energy and keeping the design small to medium allows the strength of this type to flow with purpose.

Fabric characteristics

- Soft, comfortable, and supple: These texture elements combined with a medium to soft fabric choice, works best for this type.

- Cascading and caressing structure: This Essence Type does not care for stiff structure in the fabrics they wear; they prefer soft energy movement.

- They also prefer sleeves to flow down to their wrist, no three-quarter sleeve lengths for them.

- Some structure terms: plush, soft, smooth, swooping, and relaxed.

Color

- Pure color (hues) with gray added (tones): When gray is added to the pure color of a hue, the movement of energy is evoked into a muted, romantic and nurturing color that aligns with Essence Type 2. On the artist palette and the color wheel, these colors are known as tones.

- Off-white (gray undertones): The Essence Type 2 responds to an off-white that has gray as an undertone quality to pure white. As Essence Type 1's pure white can have too much of an energy void for Type 2, the gray off-white becomes the "go-to" white color for Essence Type 2.

- Gray-black: Essence Type 2 does not gravitate to a pure black as it is too void of energy. The "black" for this type is a dark gray.

ESSENCE TYPE 3

Essence Type 3 feeds from the flowing detail of Essence Type 2 and begins its deliberate movement around the corner, before handing off to Essence Type 4. There is no mistaking the bold, rich, vibrating strength of people with Essence Type 3.

- Example: actress *Lauren Bacall* and singer *Pink*.

Essence Design Elements

- This Essence has a very determined quality of its energy.

- It picks up momentum and carries a medium to medium-high energy that showcases rich design patterns and substantial fabrics.

- It has a grounded energy that connects the person to the earth and can be heard as they walk in the direction of their purpose. When the Essence Type 3 is aligned inside out, their energy becomes crystal clear.

Design Patterns

- Medium patterns: This Essence Type feels its strength in a pattern that is not too dense and displays geometric boldness.

- Angled lines: There is nothing more determined than angled lines in a pattern! They create points and Essence Type 3 follows their internal arrow pointing the direction they choose! These lines are active.

- Squares, rectangles, and triangles: These shapes create a grounded energy that keeps Essence Type 3 close to the earth and gives them a platform of substance and volume.

- Asymmetrical: Essence Type 3 does not move too fast or too slow, this pattern takes your eye a moment to feel the messy balance and creates just the right amount of movement. This pattern also compliments the movement of the angled lines and creates an edgy feel.

Fabric Characteristics

- Tactile and visual texture: Texture, in general, attracts the energy of Essence Type 3. It reflects the bold and exotic nature. The feel of the fabric with its bumps and grain is essential to the Essence Type 3.

- Medium to heavy weight: A firm structure is important to Essence Type 3 because, with their substantial energy, they would not feel right in a soft fabric. They feel best in a medium to heavy weight material that has a firm structure.

Color

- Pure color (hues) with black added (shades): Essence Type 3 aligns with the earthy flavor of these colors. On the artist palette and the color wheel, these colors are known as shades.

- Cream-white (yellow/gold undertone): The energy of cream-white with the yellow/gold undertone adds more rich substance that aligns with Essence Type 3. A pure white does not hold the strength that Essence Type 3 needs to feel complete.

- Brown-black (rich brown with gold and black undertones): The energy of a rich brown-black brings that vibrant earthy connection that Essence Type 3 helps them feel strong. Pure black is too absorbing and quiet for this determined Type's energy vibration.

ESSENCE TYPE 4

Essence Type 4 reflects all the Essence Types and springs into an abundance of energy to bring the Essences to a full circle. Its upward movement creates wholeness and ignites the light within, before the calmness of Essence Type 1 peaks again. The energy of people with Essence Type 4 brings us home with explosive celebration.

- Example: actress *Debbie Reynolds* and singer *Miley Cyrus.*

Energy Design Elements

- With the energy of sparkling sunshine, Essence Type 4 can lift all those around them. Their design elements are the most energetic and busy with movement.

- They can go from medium-high to high design patterns in fabric choices.

- The movement of Essence Type 4 designs hops and skips to stay in tune with the path they are taking to achieve their goals.

Design Patterns

- Fun Patterns: Flowers and abstract to animated patterns appeal to Essence Type 4. Lively patterns feed their energy.

- Upward and circular lines: The upward movement aligns with the upward spiraling energy of this type.

- Stars, circles, squares and rectangle shapes: Essence Type 4 can handle the widest variety of shapes and patterns of all the Essence Types!

- Small to medium shapes: The more shapes that adorn fabric, the higher the energy. Essence Type 4 finds its strength in the movement of the shapes in a pattern. Think of polka dots; the smaller and the denser the dots, the more energy is created. When polka dots are bigger and not so dense, less energy is felt.

Fabric Characteristics

- Crisp and little texture: These elements reflect a smoother structure to keep an airy energy and allow the energy to flow outward. Too soft of a texture would make this Essence Type feel tired. It is important for this Essence Type to feel clean, light and fun!

- Light to medium structure: A little structure to hold them directs the energy so it can flow up. A crisp texture combined with a light to medium structure keeps them feeling springy and fresh. A "spring" has movement and it has structure, so it can bounce back.

Color

- Pure color (hues) with white added (tints): These are the most energetic colors that reflect the light, airy and uplifting strength of Essence Type 4. These colors on the artist palette and color wheel are known as tints.

- Warm-white (white with warm undertones): The energy of a warm-white reflects the upward movement towards the sky. This aligns with Essence Type 4. If it were a cool-white, it would reflect the downward movement towards the sea and this type would feel drained.

- No black: The energy of black drains their energy. The "black" substitute for the Essence Type 4 (we all need a dark color to wear on occasion) would be a warm navy blue or a warm, darkish gray. Essence Type 4 is a high energy and a pure black impedes the sunshine vibration that feeds the soul of this Essence.

JUST THE BEGINNING

This is just the beginning of discovering and identifying your true, authentic Essence Type. I have described, in general terms, energy qualities that are applied to clothing patterns, textures, and color choices to bring out the Essence strengths and align with the core of each type. You will have discovered a primary Essence Type, and some of you will have a close secondary Essence Type, or even a close third type. This is very important to take into consideration. Remember, you have all types within you and it is your unique formula that we want to put together to create your alignment from inside out.

When you have completed the discovery of your Essence Formula and incorporated it into your wardrobe choices, you will feel complete and confident every time you walk out your door. It is a sensory process that includes visual, kinesthetic, and auditory confirmation of your choices. You have now perfected your true Essence Formula that you can duplicate with ease. It's time to have fun in knowing that you are "in charge" of your closet!

To use your Essence Type elements, you must understand and recognize where you are right now, what you are wearing and how you are dressing, so you can start adjusting to wearing only your Essence Type. When you stick to the elements of your Essence energy, you will be in alignment and others will see it as you walk into a room. Your Essence will speak before your words are heard. The next step is to Undress the Naked Essence and explore who you really are under the personality you are currently dressing.

CHAPTER NINE

THE ESSENCE FORMULA ELEMENTS

"Essence is the core of all things; therefore, you are all things."

—STEFFI JO

To understand how you are currently dressing and the array of wonderful options open when you start dressing your Essence, let's talk about color and design. So many women get stuck on color. They might know their favorite color is blue, for example, but they're not sure what blue. Steel blue, heather blue, cobalt, cerulean… and what intensity of color, and what shade? First, know that every Essence Type can wear every color; it's just a matter of finding the right vibration in that color. We can break color into two elements: intensity and value. Intensity reflects the vibrational energy of a color, and value speaks to where a color sits on the scale of light to dark. Then, there's design—patterns, accessories, shapes, textures, weights, and more. Just as with color, these design elements carry different intensities and energies. That is what we'll explore in this chapter.

ESSENCE COLOR INTENSITY

Your primary Essence Type is your leader when it comes to your color choices. There are all kinds of typing systems for dressing that have come about through the years. A lot of them are based on your hair, eyes, and skin tones with emphasis on warm and cool colors. All of these are parts of you and you could say they all matter because they make up the whole you. It is important to remember that everything is energy; you are made of energy and every part of you is connected. Instead of looking at parts of you, we will consider the whole you at your core. Everything about your body is defined by your Essence, your energy. That is why when dressing in alignment with your authentic self, we must identify your Essence first.

Your primary Essence Type is your primary energy vibration and it aligns specifically with certain intensity vibrations of colors. It is the intensity of a color that holds a vibrational energy that matches yours and that is important. The intensity of a color is a scale of brightness to darkness. The darker the intensity of the color, the slower the vibration, and as a color slides to the brighter intensity, the higher the vibration. It is all about the energy or vibration that makes the difference for the Essence Types. The foundation of the scale is the pure color of hues. The hue itself remains very still and steadfast; when the intensity is darkened or brightened is when the energy moves.

What is identified first in the quiz is your core energy vibration. Your core vibration does not change. However, it does have a healthy state of vibration and it can become unhealthy when affected by its environment. For the purposes of dressing your Essence, I stay with the healthy vibration of Essence energy because this is where you get supported, feel your best, look your best and attract positive results.

What does all this mean in relation to the Essences? Each Type can wear most colors, they just need to be within the intensity vibration that matches their Essence Type. The color you choose to wear within an intensity is a matter of your preferred fashion style. Just because you can wear certain color intensities, does not mean you like all the colors. I stress this because some women are drawn to certain colors more than others. Personal preference and personality comes into play. For example, just because my Essence Type aligns with the brighter intensity of colors, does not mean I want to wear all of them. I prefer just to wear yellows, oranges, and blues, all within the intensity of my Essence Type.

Let's match the energy or vibration of color intensities to the Essence Types. They are characterized as hues, tones, shades, and tints. Essence Type 1 is the stillest of the energies; its vibration matches with hues. Essence Type 2 is next. Its energy starts flowing, and it is not too fast and not too slow and matches the vibration of tones of colors. Essence Type 3 is next. It has added energy, saturated more than Type 2, and it matches the vibration of shades of colors. Essence Type 4 holds the most energy; it sheds itself from the slower and more saturated colors and is matched with the faster vibration of the tints of colors.

Essence Type 1 = Hues (pure, saturated color).

Essence Type 2 = Tones (lower intensity, pure color mixed with grey).

Essence Type 3 = Shades (deeper intensity, pure color mixed with black).

Essence Type 4 = Tints (lighter intensity, pure color mixed with white).

ESSENCE VALUE SCALE

The second part of your unique Formula is the color value scale of your Essence color intensity. Not only does the character of a color's intensity fall within the four categories (hues, tones, shades, and tints), but a color can also change up and down in value, meaning from dark to light. This applies to all types except Essence Type 1, which prefers stillness over movement on the scale. Therefore, Essence Type 1's color movement does not go up or down on a scale of dark to light. When this Type moves it is from one color to another, staying within the color intensities of hues.

AN EXAMPLE OF MOVING ON THE VALUE SCALE

Here's an example of what it looks like to move on the value scale. Imagine Sarah, an Essence Type 2, who likes to wear pink. Being an Essence Type 2, her pink is a tone of pink (pink with a little grey mixed in) and this color can be called dusty pink. When she is in the mood for a darker color for an event, time of year, or simply "because," she could choose to go darker on her value scale to a dusty rose (pink with a darker grey mixed in). Both colors are pink tones; one is just a lighter *value* than the other.

There are many choices and movement in colors once an Essence Type understands her color intensity; her choices are not limited. They are only limited by her style choices. The values can be described as light, medium, and dark. The widest range of values will be found for Essence 2 and Essence 4 Types. Essence 1 does not care to move too much, and Essence 3 likes to stay committed.

The Essence value scale below represents Essence Types that are not influenced by their secondary type (more about that later):

Essence Type 1 = value scale is none.

Essence Type 2 = value scale is medium-light to medium dark.

Essence Type 3 = value scale is medium to dark.

Essence Type 4 = value scale is light to medium.

ESSENCE DESIGN ELEMENT INTENSITY

The third part to your Essence Formula is to listen to how your body feels when you wear all the other design elements. These elements can be in the pattern of the clothes, accessories, weight of the material, the shapes, textures, and more. Just as the intensity of a color and the value have an energy that affects your Essence, so do all the design elements. It is important to pay attention to the design elements of your primary Essence Type. They are the ones that will support you. Besides, you will not be attracted to designs that don't align with you, anyway.

For example, let's say you are an Essence Type 2 and the design pattern that aligns with you includes soft teardrop shapes. The intensity that is right for you is defined by how many soft, curvy shapes are in the pattern that feels good when you wear the outfit. When it feels good, this indicates that you are aligning with your Essence energy. Defining your unique formula takes attention and noticing the effects on how you feel and what you attract around you. Keeping an awareness of all factors will help you fine-tune what is right for you.

The intensity of design elements that you wear is also a matter of how much in combination of all elements: how much texture, how many shapes and patterns, etc. Do you need some of all elements or just a percentage to feel your best? The answer lies in a few factors. One is, how strong of a percentage was your primary Type compared to your secondary? If your primary had a very high percentage, then you probably won't need to pay attention to your secondary type. This means that you pretty much go with the energy level of your primary type.

For example, if you are an Essence Type 2, you will not feel good if you put on an outfit with too much pattern. Your energy ranges from flowing softly to medium. Your Essence aligns with a pattern covering your outfit up to fifty percent. When an Essence Type 2 sees an outfit that she is initially drawn to that has her pattern, she will look at it. If it is too much pattern, she will be tempted, yet her gut will tell her it is too much. If she buys it, she will take it home and wear it maybe a few times. It won't be something that she will pull on too often and eventually she will not wear it at all.

Design elements matter! They can make or break an outfit. It is important to understand what designs align with your Essence Type. It is not a matter of accessorizing an outfit with any of the latest "fashionable" items... they must first be your Essence Type. Otherwise, you are taking away from your authenticity and neutralizing your energy, which affects your attraction factor.

There's a lot involved in aligning your Essence Type with colors, intensities, values, and design elements that share your vibrational energy. We're going to balance all this in the next chapter, as we talk about bringing everything together in your unique Essence Formula. We've already touched on the idea of adjusting these elements, so you can stop dressing the mannequin and instead, give your energy to that beautiful inner girl who is desperate to be seen. Your Essence Formula will help you do that.

CHAPTER TEN

YOUR UNIQUE ESSENCE FORMULA

"Only you hold the key to your unique Essence. It's time to open the lock!"

—STEFFI JO

I believe that dressing your Essence is the next generation in the way we choose our clothing and to know that it looks good on us. The clothing industry gives us so much to choose from to fulfill our personal preferences and they give us styles from the designers of the time, there are a lot of them, and so many beautiful and fun choices! When we shop, it can be overwhelming and confusing. I like to ask, "Are you dressing you or the mannequin?" This question brings us back to remember that dressing our own Essence is the goal. It is so easy to slip into the realm of shopping overwhelm especially when the eyes are taking in many wonderful choices. It becomes important to develop a clear Essence Formula in order to identify the outfits that are really in alignment with you!

You have taken the Essence typing quiz and it has given you a place to begin developing your Formula. Let's start there! Since the quiz, I have given you information about each Essence Type, to start sorting out your Essence Formula. It's time to take a close look at what is showing up from your Essence, and what is still a bit shy about coming forward.

We are all unique and the goal is to create *your* Formula—one that you can use when shopping to choose what aligns with you.

Your quiz results will have a percentage of all the types because you have all of them within you, even if one is so small it does not show up with a result on the quiz. Your highest score is the one that I will call your primary Essence Type. Some of you will have a very strong secondary Essence Type and a few of you may need to pay attention to the third strongest type. It is important to notice what percentage the secondary or lower types play in how you feel when testing your Essence Formula.

Your unique Essence Formula is usually the highest score in the Essence quiz. It is not uncommon to have two types that are high in results. Rarely, there will be three types close in scores. Let's look at examples from two women, Lori and Karen, to see how to address more than one Essence Type in your quiz results, and when to consider including a secondary Type in your main number.

EXAMPLES OF ESSENCE TYPING QUIZ RESULT FORMULAS

Lori's Essence typing quiz results were:

- Seventy-five percent Essence Type 3,
- Twenty percent Essence Type 4,
- Five percent Essence Type 2, and
- Zero percent Essence Type 1.

Her second, third, and forth Essence Type percentages are small compared to her primary Type, so she doesn't need to consider them as much when making dressing decisions. Her Formula is: Essence Type 3.

Karen's Essence typing quiz results were:

- Fifty percent Essence Type 3,
- Thirty percent Essence Type 4,
- Fifteen percent Essence Type 2, and
- Five percent Essence Type 1.

For most women, when we get to thirty percent in a secondary Essence Type, we start to see it showing up in how her Essence wants to be seen. Since Karen's secondary Type is thirty percent, she may feel more aligned by using some of those secondary Essence elements in her expression of her inner self. Her Formula is Essence Type 3/4, then.

A third Essence Type doesn't normally need to be considered in the Essence Formula for dressing purposes. However, it is important to consider if two types come out exactly the same or really close; further reviewing may be appropriate to identify the higher type. You can do this using the flower exercise from chapter five and the journaling exercise in chapter six.

There is an influence that a secondary Essence Type can have on the Essence Formula, though. If you have a strong secondary type, as Karen did, it needs to have some attention in your Formula, otherwise you will not feel complete or whole. Your energy will not vibrate at your best.

Let me refer back to Sarah, our Essence Type 2 from the last chapter, who likes to wear pink. She is a primary Essence Type 2 and she has a strong secondary Essence Type 4. As an Essence Type 2, her color intensity is tones, her color value ranges from medium-light to medium-dark, and her design intensity is soft to medium. Sarah's authentic Essence Formula is a combination of the two types: Essence Type 2/4. Now let's add in the influence of her strong secondary type, Essence Type 4. For her to dress authentically, we need to consider her combination. Here is where her unique Essence Formula starts to take shape. She is an Essence Type 2 first and Essence Type 4 second; what this creates is faster flow to her Essence vibration.

Sarah begins her formula with her Essence Type 2 color intensity of the tone colors. The influence of Essence Type 4's color intensity of tints does not take her away from the tones. She remains with the tone colors; however, she will naturally align and be drawn mostly to the lighter color values of the tone colors. Her design element's intensity is also affected by the faster energy of the Essence Type 4. Sarah's Essence is drawn towards the busier patterns on the medium intensity end of the scale.

Every Essence Type is unique. It takes just a little shift in the intensity or value scale to notice where your authentic wholeness feels the best to you. First it is learning and becoming aware of your primary Essence Type and its strengths by itself, and then the influences that your secondary Essence Type may place upon your Essence Formula. There are many moving pieces to each Essence Type; each unique Formula is like a dance that can be learned, and it is your rhythmic movements that make it your own.

TESTING YOUR ESSENCE FORMULA

Here's a fun challenge for you! Now that you know your Essence Formula, it's time to put it into action. On a day when you feel good, take your Formula to your local department store and buy yourself a brand new outfit that fits your Essence Formula. This will include: a dress, or a top and skirt, or a top and pants; shoes; jewelry; a purse; and even lingerie and makeup! (Note: If you are not feeling your best, you risk purchasing your weakest Essence Type outfit; it's not completely you but it feels safe or nurturing or you want to hide. Buying your weakest Essence Type in clothing and accessories can become automatic or subconscious. Be careful of this happening.)

Make sure that you pay attention to your formula as you are purchasing each item. How do they work together to support your Essence? How do you feel when you wear each item separately and then together? You may encounter a salesperson or personal shopper who will try to assist you; this is fine as long as you stick to your true Formula!

How much of your other Essence pieces need to be honored with your primary Essence? That's the testing… figuring out the percentage. Are you eighty percent in your primary and twenty percent in your secondary? Few people can wear one Essence Type and feel comfortable. What do you need to support your primary color or pattern in your outfit? If you are feeling stuck with your clothing, experiment with your accessories to shift your energy. There's a definite energy in the movement and color of jewelry. For instance, Essence Type 1 is all about shiny silver because of the still energy. Type 2 is brushed silver because of the soft energy. Type 3 likes big, bold, brassy, or dark gold jewelry. Type 4 likes fun, uplifting, shiny gold. Sometimes, all it takes is one great necklace to be a game changer!

When you have your outfit picked out, find a second outfit from your closet that really isn't your Essence. Pick one night and go out in this outfit. Observe how others, particularly your friends or family, interact with you. Write down your observations in your journal. Pick a second night and go out again, this time in your new unique Essence Formula outfit. What do you notice? Chances are you will receive more attention from those around you.

If you don't notice a difference, ask yourself, "Does my new outfit fit the formula?" You can always go back and reexamine your results. You will know when you are successful with your unique Essence Formula because you will look and feel more at ease with your outfit—and others will definitely take notice. Have fun experimenting and don't be afraid to try something new!

Next, I am going to breakdown qualities of your Essence Type that are building blocks to be considered when understanding and defining your unique Essence Formula. These qualities will be used when creating your Essence Power Statement—a powerful exercise we'll do together now.

CHAPTER ELEVEN

YOUR ESSENCE POWER STATEMENT

"Your power has always been within you waiting for you to recognize the truth of who you are and to value every beautiful aspect!"

—STEFFI JO

A Power Statement is a way to claim your Essence and fully embrace it with your whole self. It is your declaration of personal truth. I found this particularly useful when connecting to my own Essence and learning to bring that understanding to dressing. I so easily got confused and overwhelmed when trying to buy clothes. In those moments, I used a Power Statement to remind me to connect to my Essence. Now, I've internalized this connection and don't rely so heavily on the prompt from my Power Statement, but it was invaluable in the beginning, particularly on days when I felt sad or tired.

I created a more purposeful Power Statement for others to use after learning about the studies on confidence and "I am" statements. Your Essence Power Statement is, at its core, a series of "I am" statements to center your attention on your true Essence. Research in this area shows that announcing to the universe that "I am… confident, strong," whatever you want to be, creates a physical shift in your body and mind at the same time. You instantly become more confident, strong, whatever you declared, through the act of vocalizing and embodying it. Tony Robbins, who is perhaps one of the most famous transformation coaches today, and other coaches and speakers across the world use "I am" statements in their work to help in the transformation process.

In your Power Statement, you will combine all the work we've done identifying your Essence Type, your Formula, and the Essence elements that vibrate in alignment with you. We'll use words that evoke self-love, along with colors, textures, shapes, and energies that empower you. Once written, this short Statement will help you remember your Essence of who you are, trigger memories of who you really are, and help you feel it in your heart. When you go shopping, your Power Statement will keep you focused and make the experience easier and more joyful. Instead of getting caught up in all the shiny objects and pretty clothes, you'll be able to sink into your energy, remember who you really are, and feel confident in what works for you. It's an affirmation that will build on your connection with your alignment and become fuel for your inner Essence.

Years ago, when I created my first "I am" statement, it was seven words: I am a loving, creative, vibrant woman. Every time I read it, the words would bring me back to who I was and why I was on this earth. Now, though, I see the value in taking this further. The Essence Power Statement I use today is longer, marries the energy and elements inside and out, and reminds me what it's like to jump into the beautiful adventure of dressing me.

To create your Essence Power Statement, take a few minutes and think about each of the following. How would you answer?

- I am a beautiful woman who expresses my inner Essence with the energy of….
- I surround myself with the energy of these colors that express my inner beauty to the outside world….
- I use these expressions of my Essence that include, design, texture and movement to strengthen my outer beauty in alignment with my inner beauty….
- I am a….

MY COMPLETED ESSENCE POWER STATEMENT

I am ***STEFFI JO.***

I am a beautiful woman who expresses my inner Essence with the energy of:

uplifting, creative, inspiring, colorful, golden-textured abundance.

I surround myself with the energy of these colors that express my inner beauty to the outside world:

Tints in the medium range of: orange, coral, pink, yellow, turquoise, mint, violet, white, and navy.

I use these expressions of my Essence that include design, texture, and movement to strengthen my outer beauty in alignment with my inner beauty:

Circles, triangles, points, polka dots, smooth, structured, crisp, lightweight to medium fabrics, and medium energy designs.

By understanding and embracing my Essence, I have empowered my true inner self to become and attract what my heart desires!

I am a creative, playful, vibrant, and inspiring woman!

I am in total alignment with who I am, inside and out, thus creating the person I came into this world to be. I am me.

Signed: ***STEFFI JO***

Date: September 25, 2000

Now, it's your turn! Pull out your journal, reflect and write out your own answers, just as I did, and create your very own Essence Power Statement. Read it every time you need a reminder of just how wonderful, unique and beautiful you are. I wrote my power statement on a 4x6 note card and carried it in my purse until I felt confident, I'd internalized its message. You can do the same!

FOR YOUR JOURNAL

My Essence Power Statement

I am [your name].

I am a beautiful woman who expresses my inner Essence with the energy of:

[Your Essence descriptive words go here. They are ones that you connect to at a deep level, the ones that fills your heart with your truth.]

I surround myself with the energy of these colors that express my inner beauty to the outside world:

[Your Essence colors go here, the ones that are your favorites, that you're creating your style around.]

I use these expressions of my Essence that include design, texture, and movement to strengthen my outer beauty in alignment with my inner beauty:

[This is where you write all the descriptive words that you love about your Essence design elements—the ones that really make a difference when you're loving what your wear.]

By understanding and Embracing my Essence, I have empowered my true inner self to become and attract what my heart desires!

[This is where you create your "I am" statement, one that stands true when you think about yourself in your happiest state at any age. This is a declaration of you. It is time to acknowledge yourself for your strengths. The words that you choose represent the real nature of your Essence energy and your spirit.]

I am in total alignment with who I am, inside and out, thus creating the person I came into this world to be. I am me.

Signed: [Your name]

Date: [The date you create this statement]

(It is important for you to sign your name and date your statement because this is confirmation to yourself and the Universe that you acknowledge the truth of who you are. This is self-love!)

REFLECT AND DRAW STRENGTH

Make it a regular practice to reflect on your power statement when you are having a tough time. Sit in a quiet room, breathing deeply, and repeat your Power Statement to yourself. This is especially helpful when you are facing a personal challenge and need to draw on your Essence strength. Surround yourself with or wear your power color(s) as a reminder of how unique and powerful you are! This strength will energize you as we move into the next part of this book and explore undressing Your Essence.

PART THREE

UNDRESSING YOUR ESSENCE

"Who have you decided to dress today? The mom, the wife, the entrepreneur, the public speaker, the nurse, the lawyer, the chef? When do you decide to dress you?"

—STEFFI JO

CHAPTER TWELVE

DRESSING FROM THE INSIDE-OUT

"The outer Personality we live and express to others is created from our Essence, but it is not our Essence."

—STEFFI JO

Are you embodying your true primary Essence? Do you dress from the outside-in or the inside-out? Think about the sum of who you are on the outside. Consider the part of yourself you have created to fit into the life you are living right now. Your life on the outside is your personality. We spend a lifetime fine-tuning ourselves, our personality, into what best fits our needs and wants for the life we live. Think back to the choices you have made about yourself as you were growing up. Your experiences shaped your views and decisions. You have either consciously or unconsciously created who you are living as today.

The concept of dressing outside-in instead of inside-out refers to the fashion choices you make. In some instances, your choices have been influenced by your experiences and expectations up to this point. You've based them on the picture in your mind of what is needed to live your life. You have made other choices without reason, just because you love something in particular. Which type of choice tickles your inner child? It is the one you have chosen for no real reason, because you just love it and want it? When it comes to your wardrobe, allowing yourself the pleasure of indulging your inner child will make you smile and feel good! It's an unconscious choice to dress from the inside-out!

STEP 1: FEEL THE DIFFERENCE

Intellectually understanding the difference between these two dressing concepts is something most of us have heard before. I am asking you to connect to feeling the difference. Think back in your life and find just one example of seeing a dress or clothing piece and gasping with delight because it was perfect for you. The first step in connecting to undressing and then dressing your Essence is remembering the energy you have had when seeing and feeling the clothing piece that you loved without reason!

I have introduced you to the concept that dressing from the outside-in is taking what the personality has created, from its experiences and what it believes about them (good or bad), to make choices in what you wear. It can be a very emotional process based on the beliefs we have created from our experiences. How many times have you been unhappy with what you wear? Can you pinpoint the core of the reason behind the unhappiness? Most of us have those times when we do not feel our best or our healthiest. Our body type also influences our clothing choices. Even when you are not feeling your best about your body, it does not mean you need to wear clothes that make you feel even worse.

Your personality has a treasure chest full of choices and even options supported by others whom you respect. In this book, I will teach you how to lead your decisions from the inside-out and support them with what you have learned from the outside-in. That is the fun part! Before you picked up this book, I imagine that you have had times, like me, where you have not felt good about yourself and the way you dress either makes it or breaks it for you. There was a feeling that dressing was "hard," and it's a dreadful feeling in times when you know you want to look your best. This book is a journey of finding the fun in exploring the best of you, recognizing who that is, and feeling the difference so it becomes "easy" to find just the right outfit for any occasion!

We are all born with natural traits that influence the way we react to the world, our environment, and our experiences. Our personality directs how we dress from the outside-in. You could say personality is a dress in itself; in the simplest of terms, it has been created to cover and protect the Essence. Through time, the personality grows and evolves from its experiences and will make decisions and choices by getting more creative. After all, it has learned new things. How about teaching your outside personality some new ways to approach your choices, based on your innate knowing of yourself, and to lead those dressing decisions from the inside-out?

What if you could check your choices against your own personal Essence Formula when you went shopping, before you spend your money? It could be your guide, at least until you feel good about all your clothing choices, and have a closet filled with only those pieces that fulfill you from the inside-out. Now there is a goal: A closet full of clothes that, no matter what you choose to wear, support you, look great on you, and feel great too! What will you be able to accomplish when you walk out your door?

STEP 2: GET UNDERNEATH

The second step to connecting to undressing your personality and dressing your Essence is to dig in and clear your mind from your outside influences, revisit the Essence typing quiz, and confirm you have your formula. From my experiences working with clients, the first time taking the quiz does not always expose the true Essence in its entirety. After all, it is not always comfortable to get vulnerable; it takes inner courage to look underneath the personality traits that run our outer lives.

It is important to respect our personality because it is our protector. You may have created a personality you are happy with. If not, you are on a self-growth, self-discovery path of improvement. You will evolve into the person you know in your heart that you need to be. The only real constant in life is change, and as you use this process of understanding your Essence, you will learn and grow to feel even more whole and complete on the outside.

Let's get more personal, and start undressing your Essence to get underneath your personality! This is where you will find your treasure, honing your Essence Formula, so you can apply it consciously and collaboratively with your outside personality. This combination helps you identify your authentic edge—your secret sauce when dressing and duplicate it in all your branding. With this knowledge, you will be dressing from the inside-out, congruent and in alignment. It helps you create that visual rapport and attraction that others see before they hear you. This is a major factor in branding you and your business.

Are you able to answer the question, "Do you dress from the outside-in or the inside-out?" Most of us will do some of each, but do you understand the difference by now? Can you identify examples of when you have made choices of what to wear from both of these directions?

The choice is always yours, and when you become aware of your Essence Formula, the choices become easier and fun to make. Remember, your clients and your audience are attracted to the real you!

STEP 3: FIND EXAMPLES

The third step is to keep diving into your Essence typing quiz and identify examples of how you have dressed from the outside-in versus the inside-out. The more you can understand your personal choices, the easier it will be to use your Essence Formula when shopping for clothing or picking out the ones you already have in your closet. Here is an example of dressing from the outside-in...

Linda is a young woman creating a career in real estate. She wants to be successful and takes note of other women who are very successful in real estate, observing how they dress. She sees a common theme among the successful women selling in the same environment and market. Linda then creates a picture in her mind, and determines how she will dress, using them as a reference. She has also received lots of positive comments about how great she looks in blue.

Linda sets out with a picture in mind of what a very successful real estate woman wears and goes shopping for just the right outfit. She finds one in blue and brings it home to wear the next day. When looking in the mirror, she sees herself fitting into her desired successful real estate woman's way of dressing. She looks good and goes about her work.

Linda hopes for some positive feedback from others about how she looks. After all, she is new and wants to do well. She also understands she is creating a whole look and feel for potential clients to be attracted to working with her. She wants them to see a professional, successful woman, who knows how to take care of them. Linda has the knowledge and skills, and loves what she does! She knows her visual impression will set the tone when beginning relationships with clients. They will either see someone they want to do business with, or they will not.

However, the feedback that day did not encompass all she was hoping to receive. She noticed that after wearing that outfit a few more times, she was not drawn to wear it any longer, and it just hung in her closet. She kept experimenting with other clothes. Sometimes she even brought home new outfits and never wore them! She could see her outfits were right for her job, but she did not always feel her best when wearing them. Something was off, and she felt like she always had to find something else to wear. Linda knew she was spending way too much time and money on figuring out a wardrobe. It became a chore to choose what to wear. She began to settle for what she thought was the right style for her.

Linda was dressing from her learning experiences and beliefs from her past. Some worked for her style and some did not. The result? She was dressing according to all her outside influences, and not based on who she authentically was on the inside. The off feeling Linda was experiencing was due to being out of alignment with her Essence. Her gut, her intuition, was trying to get her attention to let her know it was not right for her!

IDENTIFYING AN OUTSIDE-IN OUTFIT

Can you remember wearing an outfit once, then letting it hang in your closet, never to be worn again? That was an outside-in outfit that did not have enough of your Essence to draw you to wear it again. Here's how to know when you are wearing an outside-in outfit:

- You feel stiff, awkward, or more introverted;
- Your energy is drained, and you feel tired, sad, or irritable;
- People ask if you are "feeling okay" (because your energy is off, and you are out of alignment);
- You can't wait to get home to change clothes; and
- You are reluctant to be noticed and are less social.

When you are drawn to wearing an outfit, there is some element of it that is in alignment with the real you. The question is, how much? Here's how to tell when you are wearing clothes from the inside-out:

- You suddenly get a burst of energy when you get dressed;
- You smile more and feel brighter;
- You find it easy to accomplish tasks;
- Other people ask you "what's different?" because you "look good;"
- You love being noticed and are more social.

That is where the magic is! The more an outfit encompasses your Essence energy, the greater the value of shining from the inside-out. Have you ever seen someone wearing an outfit that seems too loud or too dull? That is because they are not dressing with their primary

Essence first. The primary Essence is being lost within another Essence Type that is not naturally theirs.

This type of personal exploration may be a new type of journey for you, and it may not be easy. After all, you are discovering your Essence, determining your unique Essence Formula, identifying your outside-in and inside-out outfits, and challenging yourself to grow into a more connected level of being every step of the journey. It is a fun and energizing process, but it can also be emotionally complicated. Deep, transformative work like this often takes some figuring out. In the next chapter, we will figure out which Essence Type you're currently wearing and play with some tricks to help you further tweak and feel confident in your unique Essence Formula.

As we leave this chapter, I want to remind you of the story of the Wizard of Oz. Dorothy wanted to find what was missing from her world. In the end, she found everything she wanted was back where she started, at the very beginning. She just had to remember, with new knowledge, new eyes, and new ways to understand, what she had all along! That's what this discovery process is about. Think about it like this: You are taking a walk on the yellow brick road and along the way, you stop and explore. You may find familiar information presented in a new way, or perhaps one of your stops presents new information for you to ponder. As you walk further along the yellow brick road, you notice that everything you learn starts to make sense and feels good. You are curious about where you will find your destination and what you will look like at the end of the road. Everything you will explore and learn, walking through this magical land, brings you to the discovery and the memory of a natural expression of your true self.

CHAPTER THIRTEEN

WHAT ESSENCE ARE YOU WEARING?

"To explore who you are at your core is the greatest journey you can make, and it is where you find the real you!"

—STEFFI JO

By now, you have taken the Essence typing quiz and identified your Essence Formula. You have put your Essence Type scores in order from highest to lowest. Your highest score is your primary Essence Type and how close your second, third, and fourth scores are to it will determine how strongly they influence your unique Essence Formula. This influence is important—this is the tweaking process that takes place to confirm your formula. Remember, you are not just one type; you are a combination of all of them! What elements does your Essence need to put on to feel its best on the outside? What energy elements need to be in place to showcase your Essence visually so others see you before they hear you, and invite you in?

It is important to get your formula as complete as you can. It is easy for our minds and our egos to get in the way when choosing the answers on the quiz. If you have cleared your mind of outside influences, away from the personalities you put in place for the different roles you have in your life, then you probably have your formula.

MISIDENTIFIED ESSENCE FORMULAS

Imagine a happy little girl. She is jumping all around because she loves to laugh, sing, and play games. She is doing what comes naturally; she is energetic and louder than her siblings or the daughters of her mom's friends. Her mother becomes aware that she is not behaving as the other little girls and tells her to "settle down" and behave like the other "good" little girls. The group of mothers and daughters are together again, and the little girl gets louder and jumps all around, again more than the others. The mother worries that her little girl is not fitting in and gets annoyed with her. This happens again and again until the little girl starts to lose her confidence. She starts behaving like the other little girls in order to get her mother's approval. Her primary Essence Type is a 4, the highest energy of all the types. The mother's primary Essence Type is a 2, and the other little girls are an Essence Type 2, the more mellow and flowing energy type. The mother is wanting to raise her the best way she knows how, and unconsciously wanting her daughter to mirror her own Essence Type 2 energy. She corrects the little girl's behavior constantly to mirror her own and she dresses her in clothes that she innately likes for her own energy, not the little girl's energy.

So, the little girl learns to mask her inner primary Essence energy and rely on the energy of Essence Type 2, her second strongest type, in order to get her mother's approval and love. She mirrors her mother's behavior and clothing choices. The little girl created an unconscious belief that she must behave a certain way and she must look a certain way to get her mother's love.

Some little girls will grow and rebel, and others conform because the belief becomes deeply seeded into their mindset. This little girl grew up choosing clothes that were more subdued in order to please her mother and fit in. She was dressing from the outside-in, based on a belief that she created from emotional experiences. Her primary Essence did not go away. (It never goes away.) She wore a different Essence energy of clothing on the outside than that which aligned with her authentic primary Essence on the inside. When she takes the Essence typing quiz, she answers from beliefs that are not from her innocent inner knowing.

Her results showed that her primary Essence Type was 2, and not the 4 that is her true authentic Essence Type. If she continues to dress her lessor Essence Type 2, after understanding the four Essence Types, she will feel off. She has begun to awaken and yet has not undressed enough to recognize her true Essence Type 4.

RE-TAKING THE QUIZ

Like I have said before, most of us have experienced meeting a person who has grabbed your attention somewhere. You notice that something does not quite add up and you can't put your finger on it. You see them, hear them, and watch their behavior, and something feels off. You have no real explanation for what you feel, and you decide to move on. No big deal—unless you are the other person! If you are in a business situation, that person wants your attention. They want to attract new clients or fill a workshop and make an overall good impression. Remember, the visual acceptance rule is that you have less than seven seconds to build rapport.

Undressing the Essence is about understanding the naked Essence and getting down to the real inner knowing of who you are at your core, freeing your mind from the inner chatter of beliefs, and trusting your intuition. This is about identifying the core energy of your Essence. Once you truly grasp that science has proven everything is made of energy, this opens the understanding that you are energy, and your Essence is energy. All energy does not vibrate at the same rate. The goal is to find out at what rate you vibrate and put it into terms that you can dress your unique energy, on the outside, with elements that align with your vibration—your Essence Formula!

Your vibration is the rate at which your energy moves. It's the way your mind, body, and spirit continuously shift in balance with each other and the world surrounding you. As a trained artist, I'm very attuned to the vibrations of colors and how they correlate to other things. I have a background in energy work, vibrations, and, of course, I love to dress. These things combined brought me to understand the deep healing that comes through dressing your Essence. Color is perhaps the easiest visual to understand vibration, as we can see and sense the energy of colors aligned on the color wheel.

Each color, each hue, tone, shade, and tint has its own energy vibration, and so does each Essence Type. Keeping with the idea of colors on a wheel, imagine a circle, and as you go around the circle, you are following the movement of energy. At the beginning or top of the circle are the hues. They are the truest of pure, saturated color, and as they sit at the top, they stay very still with little to no movement. As you begin to move down the right side of the circle, it takes a little more energy to flow downward. This is where the tones hang out. The movement is created by adding gray undertones to the hues. Eventually the energy flows down even more on the circle and bumps into the shades, and they take over. They have a more determined energy created by adding black to the hues, and these rich colors propel the energy around the bottom of the circle. As the shades push their energy around the bottom, the tints grab on and pull the energy upward around the left side of the circle. The tints are happy to pull the energy upward because this is their nature. To lighten up and create an uplifting vibration, the hues are mixed with white to create tints. The energy of the tints move upward and back to the beginning of the circle. This completion closes the circle and represents the wholeness of the energy within all of us.

The question is, what area of this energy circle does your primary—your true—Essence feel the happiest? Your Essence will feel more empowered and complete when it finds the answer to this question and starts to wear the corresponding energy, because you will be in alignment with your natural vibration. I have given you the example of the circle above, so you may begin to understand where colors fall into alignment with energy vibration. It is also important to understand that all design elements of textures and patterns fall into an energy vibration that can be overlaid on the same circle!

As you grow from a child into an adult, you take on roles and labels that may seem as though they define who you are at that time. These roles can come and go as your life changes or you see fit. Examples are roles like daughter, spouse, mom, employee, or entrepreneur. You find ways to fit into these roles and they may not be a true representation of that inner child's energy, passions, or dreams. They are all part of you on that energy circle... they just may not be where your true Essence is one hundred percent in alignment. Your Essence does not change. It is consistent, and the goal of feeling whole and happy is to understand and connect with the energy of where your true Essence likes to reside. Imagine having this awareness and supporting your Essence every day as you walk out the door wearing clothing with the same energy as you. It would be very hard not to feel good about yourself at some level!

Understanding this, I invite you to take the quiz again with a new perspective. See if you get new results or confirm the first results. This is a process of getting "naked and undressed." Before we move on, let the little girl come out and giggle during the process!

Undressing your Essence is the process of understanding and recognizing the core Essence energy you have been wearing, and why you wear it. The more you can sharpen your awareness of the energy you have been wearing and why, the easier it will be to make new choices that you are totally aligned with—and that help you feel beautiful!

Keep in mind that you have all the Essence Types in you, and there are a lot of outside influences that can keep you questioning what to wear when making choices, especially for a special event. If you are not feeling one hundred percent or close, you can project an Essence Type's energy that is not your strongest and make choices that really are not your best. These choices may be just mediocre, so you feel just okay. You can't exactly put your finger on why, but the clothing choice you made will probably not be your first again. You may not even wear it again! How do we make these unconscious choices that mess with our true Essence energy? Why do we wear choices that are not enhancing and aligning with that inner truth? Let's undress more of what we know and what we may not know to be true.

UNDRESSING THE INFLUENCE OF ENVIRONMENT

We are influenced by everything in our environment. Sometimes we just go along and make necessary choices to dress for the environment, without putting much thought into it. For example, if you live in the mountains and it snows, you make choices that keep you warm. You dress out of necessity. Then some will find the colors they like or the patterns they like, but still be limited in choices based on environment. The same goes for warm weather, and so on. Environment is a big factor to consider when buying clothes.

We all understand this, but how do you feel about the choices in front of you? Do you find that you have moved from a climate zone because you don't want to wear all those warm clothes, or the other way around? What is the energy of the warm clothes compared to the cooler clothing choices? All Essence Types can find what aligns with them in any environment they live. It's just that, for some, it may take more searching than for others. (I will explain more later.)

Another environment that influences our clothing choices is who we live with. Everyone, especially family, has an opinion of what looks good on us. It is usually how they want you to look and has nothing to do with what makes you feel good. We want to please the ones we love. We most often wear what they like to see on us, and we will talk ourselves into feeling good about it!

Here's another example of pleasing others. Say your spouse likes you to wear everyday-type dresses, but you like sporty clothes; it is just part of who you are, and you know this. You try to please your spouse, but something just does not feel right. You ignore it, and your behavior reflects your uneasiness of being out of alignment with your Essence energy. See? Everything and everyone in your environment is a factor in your choices! Doesn't it make sense that almost everything can influence your choices?

SUPPORT YOUR TRUE SELF

Understanding your Essence Type will help you make decisions that align best with you and your energy. The goal is to wear what you feel great putting on and walking out your door in, so you are confident you are in your best energy! When you know you look your best, it supports the way you handle your day.

We have all had those days when you just settle for wearing an outfit that you don't particularly care for, but it is all you have to wear… and you end having a terrible day! On the other hand, there are days when you feel great about how you look in an outfit… and your day is fantastic!

Your clothes do not make the person you are; however, they support you. They tell a story of how you feel about yourself and who you are on the inside. Ask yourself, *Who do I want others to see when they look at me? The real me or the role that I am playing?* People sense who you are and if you wear a costume for a role, they can feel it. That is why dressing your authentic self is important, so people sense your truthfulness and believability factor before you even speak.

It's time to ask yourself, *What Essence have I been wearing?* This is the undressing part. Become aware of who have you been dressing, so you can then learn to make adjustments and start dressing only in your authentic Essence!

CHAPTER FOURTEEN

SELF-LIMITING BELIEFS, SELF-LOVE, AND THE EFFECT ON ESSENCE

"To learn this language, one must open their hearts to themselves and let go of what does not serve their divine purpose on this earth. Love is what surrounds our growth and our happiness; it is what creates all life within ourselves and others. Love opens our hearts and our minds to hear what is important in our lives. Learn the language of the universe and you will be surrounded by love."

—STEFFI JO

We live in a society that places a large focus on body type, weight, beauty, and a myriad of other criteria. This leads to self-limiting beliefs, body dysmorphia, eating disorders, and other negative impacts on individual Essence. When you discover your Essence, you have a responsibility to nurture that Essence as you would a child. To dress your Essence, you need to first undress it and get honest with yourself. What is holding you back from shining? What still makes you nervous to step into the spotlight?

Our lives are created and lived according to our beliefs. These beliefs are what create our reality. So often we are conditioned as children to hold our Essence in or accept another version that is not really ours.

We tell ourselves things that are not true. Words are technically not thoughts or beliefs; they are representations of thoughts and have the power to shape beliefs. They are tools to remind ourselves and others of experiences. Although it is our thoughts, our beliefs, that create reality, we use words to describe our thoughts.

To some degree, words will also create a reality. We walk in companion realities. One reality is from our beliefs and one is from our words. By becoming aware of the relationship of these companion realities within ourselves, how they react and counter-react with each other, we can consciously begin to create the one reality that is in our heart—our true reality of our Essence. Words are tools at our disposal, that we can use to reshape and redesign beliefs that no longer serve us. Beliefs are our current reality that can become misaligned from the reality our heart knows to be the truth.

Notice the self-limiting beliefs created by thoughts and use words as tools to reshape and align these self-limiting beliefs with the true reality of your heart and Essence. Use positive words, positive thoughts, affirmations of love towards yourself and others, and new pathways will be made to your heart's reality. You are the one that creates the reality you live within. Choose your thoughts, choose your words and align them with the one reality you know to be your truth—your Essence. Changing beliefs therefore changes reality. It's so simple, and yet we hold on to them like our life will fall apart if we change them! What is the fear that holds us back from creating new beliefs and changing our life? FEAR is only False Evidence Appearing Real! If you want change in your life, create a new belief!

REFRAMING YOUR BELIEFS

Journaling is a powerful process that can help facilitate the shift from disempowerment to empowerment. It shifts you from pre-conditioned expectations about yourself, to learning to trust your Essence. It will not happen overnight, but with consistent effort you will have deeper insights into your blocks around fully dressing your Essence. Take out your journal and follow these steps.

Step 1. Note Your Existing Self-Limiting Beliefs

Write out a list of all your self-limiting beliefs around "showing up" in the world. For example, "In order for people to like and respect me I must always be a 'good girl.'" At some time when you were growing up, you were just being you. Then someone told you that you should be a "good girl," which made you believe you were a "bad girl." You wanted to be a good girl and so, perhaps unconsciously, decided to not do what came naturally, and instead you learned to do what you were told were the right things to be a good girl. This is how self-limiting beliefs are created. It seems a bit crazy.

Beliefs are both positive and negative. Here in this exercise, you are looking at beliefs that have held you back from being your true Essence—the ones formed when you were trying to please someone else. It may help to return to your Essence journaling exercise in chapter six and consider the moment you wrote about feeling your worst. Were there any false stories arising around your definition of who you "should be?"

Step 2. Notice Your Triggers

Write out a list of all the things that trigger each thought in your day-to-day life relating to your self-limiting belief. For example, at a time when you went shopping and saw an outfit you really loved, thoughts might have come up that a good girl would not wear a red dress, let alone red lipstick and nail polish to match! Think back to times when you felt your mood shift and see if you can identify the moment that triggered the change. Did someone say something? What did you see? These are clues that perhaps you are accommodating or trying to please someone else or a self-limiting belief of yours.

Step 3. Question Your Existing Beliefs

For each thought, ask yourself, *When did I first start believing this? At what age or during what time in my life? How was I "expected" to show up by others?* For example: "I started to think I had to 'be good' during Catholic school, after a summer spent with my conservative grandparents. People always wanted me to be quiet and mind my manners." By identifying when self-limiting beliefs began, you can begin to remember who you really are without the roles that you have played. When you get past them, you begin to connect to your primary Essence.

Step 4. Consider The Effect of Shifting Beliefs

Then ask yourself, *If I could shift these thoughts, how would I feel?* Describe how you would feel mentally, emotionally, and physically. For example: "If I wasn't worried about being seen as a 'good girl,' I'd feel relief, peace, relaxed, and grateful." Often, these feelings will be the opposite of those you currently experience. Open your heart to see these new opportunities!

Step 5. Reframe Your Beliefs

Imagine living in your highest state, free from these self-limiting beliefs. Reframe each belief to be something positive. For example: "I am safe to authentically express myself as a beautiful, respected woman, whatever lipstick, clothes, or accessories I wear." Even if these new, positive statements don't feel real, experiment with embracing them.

Step 6. Envision Your Reframed Beliefs

What do you look like in your higher state? Describe what you would wear if there was nothing that could stop you. For example: "I would wear a long, red silk dress with a V-neck, and dark red lipstick." Free your thoughts by releasing any constraints that have held you back in the past. It is okay to dream and allow the little girl inside to playfully imagine herself free and enjoying life on her terms!

Take your reframed beliefs, write them down and post them somewhere where you will see them every day. This could be your dresser, your bathroom mirror, or on the door of your closet. As you focus on your reframed beliefs, allow yourself to feel them in your body. Let them grow into a nourishing state of being. If you nurture yourself, your Essence will thrive. If you do not nurture yourself, you will never allow your Essence to fully come through into the world because you will be in a constant state of fear and resistance.

Take baby steps toward experimenting with pieces that bring you back to your authentic self. For example, if you desire to wear red but are afraid it is too "provocative," pick your Essence red and wear it as toenail polish or an accent scarf. Work your way into lipstick, shoes, and even a sweater. Keep a regular daily journal about your journey and the thoughts and feelings that come up. Forgive those who imprinted you with false beliefs and celebrate the freedom you now have in expressing your Essence.

NURTURING YOUR ESSENCE

Letting your Essence come into the world means illuminating others with your inherent beauty—beyond your body shape. Self-love is an important part of nurturing your Essence. When you are in a place of self-love, it's easy embrace your Essence and to dress it from a place of alignment. Self-love may look different for each person, but consider a few ideas:

- Eating healthy, nutritious foods;
- Moving your body to increase "feel good" endorphins;
- Spending time outdoors in nature;
- Taking a yoga or meditation class;
- Having fun and laughing more;
- Expressing yourself through dance, music, or art; and
- Getting adequate sleep every night.

Your inner world directly impacts your outer world. Take the time to reflect on your core beliefs about yourself, question them, and dare to create a brand new story for yourself. Self-love and self-acceptance go hand in hand. Dressing your Essence leads you to a time when you will no longer have the need to ask others how you look before you walk out the door, because you will already have the confidence, and know the answer.

In the next chapter, we're diving into a fun challenge! You'll take your reframed beliefs into your closet and discover the essence of the clothing you already own that aligns with your Essence. Every piece of your clothing has a close or distant connection to who you are. I'll guide you through a process of seeing that level of connection and deciding where each piece fits in your new understanding of your Essence Formula.

CHAPTER FIFTEEN

DISCOVER THE ESSENCE YOU ALREADY OWN: A 10-DAY CHALLENGE

"Down deep you already feel the truth. The challenge is, can you see it?"

—STEFFI JO

I invite you to discover the Essence of the clothing you already own in a 10-Day Challenge! This is a self-discovery challenge and it is part of undressing your Essence. It is a hands-on process to help you get intimate with your clothes and begin to understand what truly works for you in terms of energy design elements that align with your unique Essence Formula.

Most of us have clothes in our closet that we never wear. We like something in the store but then get it home, and it never sees the outside of the closet again. Or, we have an ugly sweater from a few Christmases ago that has never seen the light of day. This challenge is to help you get in your closet and find out what truly works for you and let go of the rest! You'll discover the design elements you are drawn toward, and the ones you hide behind when you don't feel your best. If you have a closet full of clothing that only supports the real you, you will never have to spend time questioning if something looks good again. You will know exactly why it works for you!

There is no mistaking that you have clothes in your closet you enjoy and love to wear. But can you identify the reasons, the Essence design elements that draw you to the clothing piece you love? Can you identify these in a way that you can use to go shopping and choose more clothing that you can love just as much?

Identifying these elements in the clothing we already love will help you hone your Essence Formula even more, so you can save time and money every time you go shopping. The more you play with this, the less frustration you'll experience in bringing home clothing you never wear again. It will be gone!

THE 10-DAY CHALLENGE

To take the 10-Day Challenge, you'll need to set aside some time to look through the clothing in your closet, plus grab a pen and paper to journal your experience.

Step 1. Pick Your Favorite Outfit

Choose an outfit you love. It will probably be one you wear more than any other, and you wish you had bought more than one of it.

Step 2. Examine The Outfit

Really look at it and decide what you like about it. Write it down. Identify as much as you can! Here are a few questions to ask yourself…

- Is it the color? If so, is it light, dark, bright, grey, a tint, a shade, a tone, or a pure hue?
- Does it have texture? Is it soft, hard, rough, or smooth?
- Does it have a pattern? If so, is it a busy pattern, a little pattern, or a big pattern?
- Does the pattern have shapes? If so, are they circles, squares, flowers, triangles or lines?

Step 3. Compare Your Other Clothes

Separate your favorite outfit from your other clothing. Now look at the rest of your clothes and compare them to the words you wrote down to describe your favorite outfit. Start adding the other clothes that match the same design elements of your favorite outfit, or most of the same elements.

a. Look for similarities. If pieces of clothing have fifty percent or more of the same design elements you wrote down, start hanging them together. Leave the outfits that have less than fifty percent of the elements at the other end of your closet (out of the way for now).

b. Now organize the outfits. Place clothing with a high percentage of similarity to your favorite outfit (including color) next to each other in a section of your closet. Hang pieces with fewer similarities together in another section of your closet, further away. You will probably start to see a pattern of similarity emerge. Make notes of what you notice!

Step 4. Compare Your Closet to Your Quiz Results

Go back to your Essence typing quiz results. Does your favorite outfit match the design elements of your highest scoring Essence Type? If not, which Essence Type does it reflect? You might want to review the quiz again. We are drawn to our Essence Type elements, but it is the order we get mixed up. You may be dressing your second strongest Essence Type, and that could be why you find some frustration with your clothing choices. Follow the process and you will find your Essence Formula.

Step 5. Focus on Your Favorites

Wear only the clothing pieces in the favorite section of your closest for one work week! For the five days, only wear the pieces that you placed aside with your favorite outfit in step 3. Don't wear anything that didn't make it into the favorite section.

a. Journal about your experience for these five days. How did you feel? What did you notice? Was it easy? Did anyone comment on how you looked? Write anything you notice in your journal. Everything that you notice within is important; it is your intuition speaking for your Essence. These are all clues to your unique Essence Formula.

b. Write down anything you noticed about the effect your clothing choices had on your day.

Step 6. Focus on Your Least Favorites

For five days, wear only the clothing pieces left over that did not make it to the favorite section of your closest! Stick to the pieces you placed away from your favorite in step 3. Don't wear any other outfits!

a. Journal about your experience for these five days. How did you feel in your non-favorite clothing? What did you notice? Was it easy? Did anyone comment on how you looked? Write anything you notice in your journal. Everything that you notice within is important; it is your intuition speaking for your Essence. These are all clues to your unique Essence Formula.

b. Did what you wear have an effect on your day? Record that in your journal, too.

Step 7. Compare Your Notes

Compare your notes from both weeks. What were the differences between them? Which week did you enjoy more? Use the descriptive words from step 2 and write them down.

a. It is important to write down the design element words. Did you feel better in pieces that were textured or smooth? Did you feel better in pieces that were bright or muted? You will use these words later in the book.

b. Continue to keep a journal as you fine-tune your Essence Formula. It will be important to refer to later on in this book. You can use these reflections to tweak your personal Essence Power Statement that we created in chapter eleven, so it remains a powerful reminder of your Essence whenever you are shopping and choosing your next outfit!

At this time, you might have a pretty good sense of your Essence Type and, by taking the 10-Day Challenge, you should have further confirmed your Essence Formula. You may notice you have a strong secondary type, or you may feel great in just your primary. You are now ready to begin dressing your Essence by shopping and seeing the magic happen!

PART FOUR

DRESSING YOUR ESSENCE

"When you dress your Essence, it is a declaration of self-love. It is your time to shine and declare that you are ready to attract your greatest desires!"

—STEFFI JO

CHAPTER SIXTEEN

DON'T GET LOST IN THE PROCESS

"When you know and connect to your Essence, you create a map of awareness that is always with you to call upon when looking for your true north."

—STEFFI JO

You have come so far in your self-development and growth; you have come to accept yourself and embrace the real you. Why would you not allow the world to see your self-confidence? I still catch myself, at times, when I get caught up in wanting to make a good impression and be accepted in a new situation, but I remind myself that putting my best foot forward (literally) means staying aligned to my Essence. As you become more in tune with your core Essence, it will become easy for you to distinguish between dressing your Essence and dressing a role that you live.

With all the choices we have surrounding us everywhere, it is easy to get lost in the process of finding outfits that bring out the best in you, instead of something generic that hangs on a mannequin in the stores! There are so many different types of clothes for every season, beautiful colors and textures, not to mention sales people ready to help you. The choices are endless, not only in the stores but also online. So, how do you not get lost? How do you stay focused on what is just right for you, so you stop spending money on clothes that you wear one time or never return?

It sounds like it could be simple to remember and focus on what you are shopping for, whether it's an event, work, a date, or anything else. However, have you ever gone shopping with purpose, knowing what you are looking for, but could not find anything, or you found all kinds of choices, but they just weren't quite right? You probably felt exhausted! It was enough to make your mind spin. After looking at all the choices, you left not remembering what type of outfit you really wanted. Then, there are those times you find something that just pops out at you, and it is perfect. It gives you hope to keep trying and to get through the times that exhaust you.

What if, by understanding your unique Essence Formula and following your Essence Power Statement, you could stop the frustration and know exactly what is great for you, every time you need to get something new? Could that make your life a little easier? Could you save money if you are not buying outfits just to get something? Fine tune your Essence Formula until it feels the best and you look outstanding. This is the key to not spending money on clothes that do not make you happy in the long run! This is when getting lost in the process stops.

Understanding your Essence Type and all your Essence elements is when your unique, secret Formula is unveiled. Using your Essence Formula supports your dressing for success in all areas of your life. If you do not want to get lost in the overwhelm of information and choices, then you learn how to navigate. You use your Essence Power Statement as a map, so to speak. Your Essence map will keep you on course! It is just like anywhere you go to for the first time; you need directions. You may need directions for a few times before you have memorized your way. If you have not visited your destination for a while, you may need a refresher. Then, there are those times that you may want to find a new route because you have changed something in your life, and want to venture into new territory. When this happens, you revisit your Essence Formula and Essence Power Statement, and you tweak the map for your new direction.

BEING ALIGNED WITH YOUR ESSENCE FORMULA

By now, you have taken the Essence typing quiz, settled in on your Essence Type, identified your Essence Formula with your key design elements, written your Essence Power Statement, taken the 10-Day Challenge, and tested your formula along the way. You probably feel good about your result and are trying different ways to express your Formula and confirm your results. Making sure that you are one hundred percent aligned with your Essence Formula is the first step in not getting lost.

Your unique Formula is the core energy you express from your natural, instinctual self, and it does not change. If you do not feel one hundred percent positive you have your Formula that fits, then you may still be identifying with other parts of you that you have put in place. For example, if you are totally into being a great business owner, wife, partner, or mother, you could see these parts as the real you and not connecting with your true Essence, therefore creating a misalignment between the outer you and the inner you. When we immerse ourselves in the different roles we take on, we tend to have a picture of what that looks like in our mind, and if we want to be great at it we seek to model that picture we have created in our mind. These roles are not your true Essence; they are created on top of your Essence. They are what we surround ourselves with, and sometimes these roles become so embedded that we define ourselves as such.

A woman may think, *I am a mother*, or, *I am a wife*. The reality check is that yes, you have become a mother, but you were not born a mother. Your Essence Formula is a tool that helps you remember your true Essence and feel aligned inside and out. It helps you feel congruent and at home with yourself, and when you do, you will notice when you are out of balance. When you feel something is off or incomplete, your mind, body, and spirit are not working in unity. Areas and systems in your business and life will not work as well or as successfully as they could, and you will feel stuck, unable to move further. The out of balance feeling comes when you know the difference between being aligned with your true Essence and masking it by dressing over it with one of your outside roles.

To get back into alignment, you need to let go of the mask and reconnect to your true Essence, knowing you can continue to hold the roles of mother, spouse, entrepreneur, or whatever is meaningful to you, while honoring your true self. Not only can you embody your Essence while still holding space for the identities you care about, but you can more fully embrace those identities when you connect to them from the place of your Essence.

This reminds me of the work by philosopher Martin Heidegger, who is widely considered one of the most important philosophers of the twentieth century. Stanford University said, "His ideas have exerted a seminal influence on the development of contemporary European philosophy." When I trained to be a coach, I read a commentary on his works by Hubert L. Dreyfus called *Being-in-the-World*, and I found it profound. Dreyfus explains Heidegger's idea that we can all "be" things to the outside world, but "beingness"—the very thing that makes us human beings, is on the inside. Almost a century ago, Heidegger was talking about this idea that is essentially Essence.

You can feel out of balance when you act from the energy of the things you are to the outside world—the things we can "be," instead of our "beingness." An example is when you dress for an environment, instead of bringing your Essence into that environment. I see this all the time! You look at where you are going, a formal affair, or a beach vacation, for example, and you let that determine your clothing choices, instead of looking at how you can apply your Essence to your clothing choices first and then choosing what is appropriate for the environment.

When you are invited to a formal affair, you may reach for a black dress because that is acceptable for the event. But then you are dressing for the environment, not for your Essence! When you put your Essence first and make choices for the environment from only what is aligned with your Essence, you bring your Essence into the environment, and this allows you to embody your true beingness wherever you are. Even though it seems appropriate, I won't wear black to a formal affair. I am an Essence Type 4 so tints are most aligned with my energy, and black is not a tint. I might wear dark gray, then, and having worked through chapter nine and played with color values and intensities, I know the range of gray I feel best in.

You can bring forward different elements of your Essence depending on your environment. I used to be a stay-at-home mom and now I'm working in the corporate world, so I'm dressing for another situation but still drawing from my unique Essence Formula. My Essence didn't change when I moved from working inside the home to outside. My Formula didn't change. I just started to apply it differently, to stay aligned within my new environment. My choices evolved to reflect that I wasn't running after a toddler anymore, so it was easier to wear skirts and high heels. I chose skirts and shoes that had my Essence elements, and I felt just as whole in this new style as I did wear jeans and sweaters at the moms' group.

Those jeans and sweaters were my Essence Type, but they didn't fit where I was in the corporate world, so I shifted my style while continuing to dress my Essence. The key is that I didn't look at what other women in the corporate world were wearing and try and dress the same, and I didn't choose what looked good on a mannequin in a store window. I chose design styles based on my Essence, and then made sure it was appropriate for my environment. I adjusted how I wore my Essence and gave visibility to my business by being authentic.

You can do the same thing. You can put your Essence into any environment you choose. You can style your Essence elements to create a wardrobe you love, and a business brand that your ideal clients instantly connect with. As you grow your work, you can evolve your style and branding choices to align with where you are, while always being one hundred percent connected to your Essence. That is the beautiful connection that will attract people to working with you, wherever you are at in your journey.

OWNING YOUR TRUE ESSENCE FIRST

There is another step in not getting lost in the process: You must own your true Essence first. By that, I mean you must know it deep down, and have no doubt that you feel it and see it in your actions. You remember it as being a constant part of you since you were a little girl.

Your Essence Formula is your map to expressing your true Essence, so others can know and see your authenticity, before you even speak! It is normal from time to time to take a detour and get lost. I see those times as a nudge to go back and review your Essence Formula. Ask yourself if it needs to be fine-tuned. Perhaps it is just time to reconnect to your Essence and remember who you are and how do you want to be seen in this world. A woman who shows up in her true strength, from the inside-out, by owning her authentic Essence, will feel her unshakable ability to move forward and attract what she desires. The best part is everyone around her will know it too. I like to say that when you dress your Essence, it is a true expression of the real you, and you will be seen before you are heard!

CHAPTER SEVENTEEN

NAVIGATING THE ENDLESS COLOR WHEEL

"Believe in your Essence and all that you are. Know that the Essence within you can overcome any obstacle outside you."

—STEFFI JO

When it's time to revamp your wardrobe, it is smart to arm yourself with your Essence Power Statement and begin with the most basic part of dressing your Essence: color. We're going to spend some time talking about color because I've seen a lot of women get stuck here. It's natural, given that most women have never been trained to understand the intricacies, but it's a shame, because color can be really fun!

Every color has its own vibration, and we can feel this as we work our way around the endless color wheel. It can sometimes seem like the color wheel has so many choices that it's overwhelming, but when you approach it from a centered energy, standing in your understanding of your Essence, the choices become empowering! Women aren't usually encouraged to dig deep and feel the vibrations of the different types of blue, for example, to understand which resonates the most with them. Their mother might have said, "Blue looks nice on you," and so they look for blue without truly understanding it. But before we get to blues, or greens, reds, whites, and so on, let's start with what we understand to be the "staple color" of all wardrobes.

THE MOST COMPLICATED COLORS

Black is defined as being all colors in the art world. In the energy world, it is void of all colors. Black goes with everything, right? Is it an easy color to work with? Nope! Black is complicated! It is emotionally charged, which creates a very full and heavy sense of energy, emoting stillness with little vibration. It is all encompassing and can surround a person with a sense of safety. It is also a cloak to hide behind. It has been misunderstood because it contains a lot of emotional energy; it absorbs the surrounding light and, for some, when worn, it hides the light from within.

If you are the Essence Type that aligns with the strength and weight of black, it will contain your elegance in a way that enhances your presence. Your energy will shine like black patent leather, attracting the eye of those around you. If your Essence Type does not align with black, you will be hidden and fade into the background. It will be as if you are telling others, "Leave me alone. I do not want to be seen. I just want to blend in or 'fit in.'" The absorbing qualities of black are fascinating, partly because of the psychological emphasis that is placed on its value in the fashion industry. For some, it is empowering. For others it creates a barrier to hide behind. Every Essence Type has their own "black," but there is only one Type that is energized by a true, full on black. One Type finds her strength in a muted black, which is known as gray. Another Type aligns her energy strength with a rich brown. Grays and browns both have undertones of black, however, they are not black.

One Essence Type will use other colors for their dark color clothing that is anything but black! Most of us have a black color in our closet for certain occasions or activities. It's important to know is it a color that strengthens or weakens your energy. Learn to use colors that align and enhance your Essence as a tool to support your life and goals. Now, let's talk about the very opposite of it.

White is defined as being void of colors in the art world. In the energy world, it is all colors, like a prism. White is also complicated! It can be as cold as ice and create a barrier, or it can be the lightest, most freeing and uplifting of all the colors worn.

The nuances of white are fascinating to me. Just when you have a white color picked out, you put it against another white and it changes color, perhaps to a light gray or yellow. Whites are unique and, just as with black, white is not the best energy for all the Essence Types.

THE RIGHT COLOR FOR YOU

Here's a scenario: You are wearing a blouse in blue, for instance, and every person you meet tells you, "I love that color!" Yet you don't feel great, even though you like blue. You actually feel a little off. What's up with that? Do they really see you or just the color? Should you be feeling better than you do because others are saying they like the color you are wearing? Not at all! The blouse has a nice blue color and you are not feeling your best wearing it. This combination is telling you it is not the right blue for you! If it were, you would love it and feel great wearing it! Others who tell you they love that color (and not that you look great) are actually saying that they are attracted to that color of blue and want to wear it themselves. It is not about you! There are lots of different blues in the world, and one size (or color, in this case) does not fit all.

The right color for you is based on your energy, your Essence, personality, and style. The right color for you will match your energy first, your Essence energy, which is the core of your authenticity. To know your true blue, you must consider who you are, inside and out! For example, a brighter blue, one that has white undertones, would be a much better fit for someone with a naturally cheerful and playful energy, for instance. A blue with gray undertones will bring that person's energy down; it would make them feel tired or not quite their cheerful self. It would be a mismatch of their authentic core energy and the energy of the color. When you wear the right color for you, there is an alignment of energy and you are in sync.

It is my experience that most people tend to see colors as one kind, ignoring a range of different qualities and values to choose from. A high energy personality aligns with a different blue than that of someone with a more mellow personality. Once you understand your

Essence energy and the colors that vibrate as you do, a whole new and easier way to go shopping for clothes opens up!

Below, I'm listing the main qualities of a few of the most popular colors women wear. The combination of elements, texture, line, pattern, weight, and so on, will make for the perfect outfit that empowers you and brings the best of the real you forward. It only begins with color, as that is something, we all see first. Besides that, it is just plain fun to talk about color!

A FEW POPULAR COLORS

Red

It is often said that red is the "power" color and it attracts the eye almost immediately. Psychology tells us that red (consciously or unconsciously) is either worn in preparation to go into battle, or when one is feeling happy and confident and wants the world to know. This color is full of energy! A small amount of red can draw attention and make a positive statement. On the other hand, too much red can overpower a room with an aggressive feeling. It is a highly visible color and knowing which red vibrates in tune with your Essence Type can empower you in a positive manner. It is to your advantage to wear the red color that is just right for your Essence Type. By wearing any other red besides the one that is in harmony with your Essence, you could create adverse reactions from those around you; you could be seen as aggressive, harsh, and unapproachable.

Fine-tuning your eye to pick out the red for your Type will help you be successful when strategically wearing this powerful color. Celebrating the holiday season with your red dress will have a whole new meaning! Which one is your Essence red: A pure hue, fully saturated red, a muted red, a rich red, or a light red? The answer lies within understanding the energy of your Essence and how it affects your choices in color.

Blue

This is a color that everyone seems to relate to, and most people say it is their favorite color. The lighter to medium-dark blues are soothing and calming colors. People will gravitate towards blue when they need some relief from the intensity of a busy environment. It is also a color that brings clarity in thought and communication. It is a color of reflections and a color that can connect us to the gentleness within. Blue, when worn, is also seen as an invitation to connect with others.

On the dark side of blue, deep navy has a confident energy that is authoritative, but its darkness does not settle down all Essence types. For some, it brings strength and for others, it feels heavy and draining. The key for the overall positive aspects of blue that we gravitate towards is to find your true blue. It can be warm or cool, it can be light or dark, it can be a pure natural blue, but it needs to be your Essence blue. One more thing… almost everyone looks good in a pair of blue denim jeans!

Green

Green is a very restful, balanced, and grounding color. It is the color of the heart energy chakra. When the eyes see green, they can rest because no filters are needed to decipher the color. When wearing the green that is connected to the energy of your Essence, there is a sense of harmony for both you and those who see you. Green has its lightness and darkness the same as every color. I like to think of the earth and her many colors of green, and the healing that being out in nature can bring to all of us. Light greens in a meadow have a higher energy than the dense forest greens of the mountains.

Wearing the right green for you is very supportive and inspiring. For those whose Essence aligns with the light greens, it connects with their youthful energy. The true green Essence type connects with their self-confidence. Other muted greens will support the generosity of their wisdom and understanding. There is a very positive side to wearing green for all the Essence types when they are in a good state of mind. I also love the fact that green is the color of abundance!

White

The Essence Type that can wear a full strong black will also feel her strength in the starkest of whites. A full, stark, winter's white reflects the light and creates a shield that holds her energy inside and still, just where she feels the best and others can feel it. The stark, reflective, winter's white is very important to this Type because it brings balance to the absorbing barrier of the black that she also finds her strength when wearing.

On the other side of the reflective white (totally void), is the warm, inviting white—the one with undertones of the sun. The Type that aligns with this warm white finds their spirit uplifted with its energy. It is infectious to those around her. Following the prism of colors to the cooler side presents another white, a cool white. This white has a more calming energy, and the Type that is most aligned with this white feels her strength steady. Those around her will feel the nurturing effects of her energy. There is one Type that does not feel an attraction to wearing white. Their energy is closer to the earth, and they find the white that they feel best in is a rich cream. Her strength feels grounded when wearing this cream white, although not too much of it.

It is true that the choice of wearing black or white is an easy dressing decision. We are conditioned to wear black or white by traditions, fashion, and the clothing industry. Take notice of the reasons you have chosen to wear black or white, and how have they made you feel about yourself. If you are an Essence Type that is not energized by them, I want you to know that there is life after black and white. You just need to understand your Essence Type and what it looks like to substitute other colors for them.

WEARING YOUR COLORS ALL THE TIME

We have been talking all about identifying and wearing our Essence colors. Once we internalize that concept and understand the importance of it, the follow up question is always this: How do I go about wearing only those colors that align with my energy one hundred percent of the time?

The truth is, it's a process of conscious choices, and you learn how to make the best choices when your default options are not available to you at that time. There are so many factors and considerations that go into what we choose to wear each day and why. Truthfully, the goal is to have only those colors and designs in your closet that support your Essence Type. Overall, go with your gut feelings! If you do not feel you look great in the color, you put on and just can't put your finger on it… don't wear it! If you want to understand more about why you can feel it and can't seem to find the words to describe it, perhaps learning more about your Essence Type will help you. Then, you may never need to ask, "Does this color look good on me?"

At the end of the day, can you create a closet full of only your Essence colors and design elements? Yes, you can. I will say that it is a process that takes time. Unless you have a ton of money, your clothing budget may not allow you to get rid of all the clothes in your closet that don't work for your Essence Type! You will also go through a fine-tuning process, learning and growing, so why not build from your current favorite pieces? Lastly, it depends on what is available to you where you shop, what is in stock, and how easy it is to find the right resources for your style and type.

Finding those resources is what we will explore in the next chapter. Now that you understand your Essence, we will talk about how to shop with your Power Essence Statement, which is a process that starts before you have even entered the store. We will explore grounding yourself and connecting with that little girl within as you prepare to shop, how to make choices when you are in the mall or store, and what to do when you can't find clothing that is one hundred percent within your unique Essence Formula.

CHAPTER EIGHTEEN

SHOPPING WITH YOUR POWER ESSENCE STATEMENT

"The illusion, the 'box,' we find ourselves living within is only our mind's fear of being seen."

—STEFFI JO

I want to make shopping easy because sometimes, it can feel really overwhelming. When I started helping women show themselves through their clothing, we'd go shopping together. I'd stand in the corner of a store, cup of coffee in hand, waiting while they'd walk around and choose outfits. They'd select a top and pants or a dress, bring it over to me, and we'd critique the clothes together. But I noticed my women would quickly get confused. They'd be overwhelmed by all the shiny objects, and forget what aligns with their Essence. It was really easy for them to spiral, and that's no fun for anyone.

That's why I started working with the Essence Power Statement—the declaration of personal truth we created in chapter eleven. When you go shopping and see all the choices available, your Essence Power Statement will bring you back to focus and help you remember who you are. I encourage you to return to the journaling exercise we did around your Essence Power Statement. If you need to tweak it to reflect your unique Essence Formula, now is the time to do that. As a reminder, here is my Essence Power Statement.

*I am **STEFFI JO**.*

I am a beautiful woman who expresses my inner Essence with the energy of:

uplifting, creative, inspiring, colorful, golden-textured abundance.

I surround myself with the energy of these colors that express my inner beauty to the outside world:

Tints in the medium range of: orange, coral, pink, yellow, turquoise, mint, violet, white, and navy.

I use these expressions of my Essence that include design, texture, and movement to strengthen my outer beauty in alignment with my inner beauty:

Circles, triangles, points, polka dots, smooth, structured, crisp, lightweight to medium fabrics, and medium energy designs.

By understanding and embracing my Essence,
I have empowered my true inner self to become
and attract what my heart desires!

I am a creative, playful, vibrant, and inspiring woman!

I am in total alignment with who I am, inside and out, thus creating the person I came into this world to be. I am me.

*Signed: **STEFFI JO***

Date: September 25, 2000

If you haven't already, I want you to write your Essence Power Statement on a note card or a nice piece of paper, capturing it as a portable affirmation that can accompany you around the mall and into the dressing room. You can keep it in your purse until you've learned to internalize its messages and become more comfortable sinking back into its energy. We all need these reminders occasionally, so pull your note card or special paper out of your purse, and remind yourself what a beautiful person you are, and what's it's like to dress you.

THE TWO SIDES OF SHOPPING

The most stressful shopping situations are usually when you know you need a pantsuit for a meeting in two days, or you know you need a dress that matches the color your daughter chose for her wedding. The pressure is on and there is all kinds of emotional energy wrapped up in finding the right outfit, because the upcoming event means something and you desperately want to look—and, more importantly, feel—your best. Sadly, those are usually the times when it feels impossible to find something great. You leave the mall exhausted and drained, with an outfit that's kind of okay, you suppose—or no outfit at all. I've even come home crying, thinking, I can't do this. I can't find something. I'm so lost or confused.

On the other hand, we've all had a moment when you go out and you aren't really looking for something specific, but you find a top you love. It just seemed to jump off the rack at you! You didn't even know you wanted something like that, but now you can't imagine your wardrobe without it. Wearing it makes you feel warm and lovely and energized, like you can take on anything.

Unfortunately, the first experience is far more common. All the time women go out and can't find what they're looking for, and maybe part of the reason is that they go shopping when they don't feel good about themselves. Then, it's easy to get frustrated and overwhelmed, forget what you wanted, and feel disappointed. This is where we spent the last two chapters talking about not getting lost in the process and navigating the endless color wheel. I wanted to prepare you to rise above these common shopping struggles. With the knowledge from this book and your Essence Power Statement in hand, you're far less likely to have these frustrating experiences and, even if you do slip into them, you will have the power to bring yourself back to a place of ease and enjoyment. You will be able to sink back in, breathe, read your declaration, remember who you are and what works for you, and return to shopping with a refreshed, light energy.

A GROUNDING MEDITATION

One way to sink into that energy is to guide yourself through a grounding meditation exercise. You can do this when things start to feel confusing, but even more wonderfully, you can do this in your car, before you even walk into a store. It will clear your mind and help you get back in connection with your Essence, so you can enjoy every moment of shopping. It will help you forget about the roles you play and get the best results from your day. Read the meditation below and follow along at your own pace, fully embodying your imagination as you delve into the exercise.

Soften your eyes, relax your shoulders down, and take a deep breath in, and out, in, and out. Feel the weight of your arms by your side and let every muscle melt into softness. Breathe in, and out. Take your mind back and remember yourself as a child. Think of that innocent time when you played happily on the playground with your peers, your friends. Where were you? What did it look like? What smells were on the air? Remember the games you played. What were you doing? Connect with that beautiful, innocent child. She is you. Were you quiet, chatty, full of laughter, or serious? What did others say about you, as that little girl? Were you the leader, or did you sit back. Look into your heart and trust your first responses.

When you've connected with that innocent little girl, gently bring your mind back to this moment. You're sitting in your car, ready to go shopping. You're looking for an important outfit, and you want success. Take another deep breath in, and out, and remember that little girl who played so happily. You're going to bring her inside the store with you! She's going to feel the sun on her face as she comes shopping with you. Her eyes will light up when she sees that outfit, the one you're looking for, and she will giggle and laugh with joy. She will overflow with fulfillment in the beauty of your find. Breathe in her energy.

Gradually, when you feel ready, pick up your Essence Power Statement, and read it through. Ground back into your Essence and embody it. Now take your Essence Power Statement in one hand, your beautiful, inner child in the other, and go shopping.

WHAT IF YOU CAN'T FIND YOUR FORMULA?

As you walk around the store, you may feel like none of the clothes are completely your Formula. The ones that do have some of your Essence elements may also have some that don't. So should you hold out for something that only has your Essence elements, or should you accept something you like, even if it's not exactly there? How can you make it doable?

I look at it like a formula of percentages and how I feel walking out the door. An outfit might be one hundred percent in your Formula, eighty percent, fifty percent, or five percent—or anywhere in between. There is no magical equation to calculate an outfit's percentage; you look at the elements—its color, intensity, and design—and get a feel for how strongly it aligns with what you declared in your Essence Power Statement. Since there are so many choices out there and since you are unique, it is unlikely you will find outfits that are one hundred percent your Formula every time you shop. That would be perfect, but I am afraid that perfect is not out there, especially when you only have three hours to find an outfit for your event tomorrow.

So then the question becomes, what percentage will you accept? What is your comfort level? For myself, I know I can't wear less than seventy percent my Essence, or I won't feel comfortable. So if I am in a hurry, I will go to a department store, because they have a lot of choices, and I will choose the best outfit I can find that feels like it is at least seventy percent of my Essence. That is how I deal with the pressure of time. If I have more time, I can shop slowly and deliberately, and find an outfit that is eighty percent, ninety percent, or more.

It also depends on where I am going and what am I doing. For instance, if I am going to be on stage speaking at an event in front of a big group of women, I will want to dress one hundred percent in my Essence colors and design elements. If I am going to the gym and I am at seventy percent or better, I am okay with that (although I am always on the lookout for gym wear that gets me as close as possible to my one hundred percent Essence energy). Ideally, of course, I would love to have one hundred percent of my Essence energy in all my clothing, but I am comfortable wearing a lower percentage when I am sweating on the treadmill. I do not want to make this a big deal in my life. Life is busy and flexibility is freedom.

Have you ever tried to be one hundred percent happy or positive all the time? There are so many moving parts to life, it is impossible to stay in one place. Changes go up and down in nanoseconds! The Universal Law of Change is always at play, even within us and our energy. The key is to be flexible, and this will free your mind to find other ways to achieve the outcome you are looking for. Your flexibility in dressing your Essence comes with understanding your unique Essence Type and your Essence percentage range that helps you feel great to outstanding within. Is it from seventy to one hundred percent, eighty to one hundred percent, or sixty to one hundred percent? You make the choice!

YOUR LITTLE ESSENCE DRESS

Now that you've explored dressing your Essence, let's revisit the concept of the little black dress that we discussed way back in chapter one. Does the little black dress support and bring out your best qualities? Are you truly seen? Are you seeing the results you desire when you wear your little black dress versus when you are wearing your Essence? Now that you have read and experimented with this information, brought awareness, and experienced your Essence Types, can you guess what your Little Essence Dress (LED) is, and how it differs from the little black dress? Your LED is any dress that aligns with your primary and secondary Essence Types, and supports your core energy!

This means your ideal dress may be any color of your primary Essence Type that you love, with any of your Essence Type design elements. Your LED will always make you feel unique, free, and joyful. When your wear your LED, you are lighting up, dressing up, and revealing your authenticity instead of hiding it in the dark and conforming in the standard, "expected" dress. The facets of your inner beauty—your personality—are always brought out gracefully when you wear your LED. Let's journal to explore your ideal LED.

LED JOURNALING EXERCISE

Describe a dress you have recently worn as part of your Essence journey that made you feel authentically you, like it was "made for you." (If you haven't found one yet, please take a trip to your local department store and play dress up!)

- What color is it? Is there more than one? What is its value? Is it light, medium, or dark?
- What material is it? Is it soft, stiff, shiny, thick, or sheer?
- Describe any adornments or accessories on the dress (for example, buttons or lace).
- What is the cut and shape of the dress? What kind of neckline does it have? Is it rounded or V-neck?
- How do you feel in the dress?
- When you look at yourself in the mirror when wearing this dress, what do you notice about yourself?

Take some time to reflect on your dress. Look at all the ways it specifically highlights you through color, cut, accessories, and so on. You will know when you have found your LED when it encompasses all your most important Essence design elements and when it feels like a part of you—so natural, you never want to take it off! When you can dress your Essence and express your Essence, that is when the magic happens.

CHAPTER NINETEEN

WHEN THE MAGIC HAPPENS

"Expressing all of who you are is expressing your magic!"

—STEFFI JO

Every human is unique, and to me, that means every human is magical and a miracle. There is something to be said for the miracle of the human body that grows and heals itself on every cellular level. It goes beyond the physical; it is the energy that our body houses that cannot be dismissed. Not only has science proved that everything is made of energy, it is also faith in the spiritual sense that tells us there is more to us than we can see. As a little girl, I could see our differences and I could feel our connectedness. There was something incongruent and confusing about the inconsistency of seeing one thing and feeling another. *Why?* That was my question. *What is the truth?*

The metaphor "don't judge a book by its cover" became real to me. The truth was obvious after searching my own soul and asking questions within. My initial conclusion became: We are who we are on the inside, and we only allow the ones we trust to see beyond the dress we wear on the outside. This belief was a little girl's way of protecting herself when she was not confident others would accept what was on the inside. It was also a time of self-discovery, trying to understand who she was, and trying to love herself for it.

Growing up, I remember believing "timeless beauty" was a description of beautiful movie stars like Audrey Hepburn, Grace Kelly, and Marilyn Monroe. True, there is a simple beauty that the eye can behold forever, but what is the attraction that stays in a little girl's dream? The key word to explore is "attraction." This is the energy that you feel towards something that pulls and connects you to what you see. It stays with you because you have the same energy within you— "like attracts like." Noticing what you are attracted to gives you information about your true Essence and the energy you are made of.

THE MAGIC OF TIMELESS ESSENCE

Your Essence is a strong energy force that, if understood and embraced, can become your magic, your timeless beauty, or, as I will expand more upon, your timeless Essence. It brings tears in my heart when I speak about timeless Essence being the beauty that every little girl is truly seeking during the self-discovery of who she is as a person and as a woman. The Essence of who you are is your timeless beauty, and to know this is your freedom to grow with self-awareness that results in self-confidence. A little girl's magic is her Essence shining for all to experience. A woman's greatest gift is giving of herself from the heart of her Essence. The more you can connect and recognize your Essence, the greater you will experience a life that you are here to create and love.

I have been asked many times: Does your Essence style change? Yes, your Essence style can change, however, your Essence does not change because this is your core self. It's the way you were born. We all come into this world with our own unique set of qualities. Like snowflakes, we are unique and there is no one else exactly like us in the world. It is also important to remember that when we are born, we are pure, innocent beings with no thoughts about anything other than the feelings of what we are now experiencing in our new environment. Our Essence is the innocent, pure energy that comes together in a unique pattern (as in a snowflake). It forms the basis for who we become. The Essence is the core energy that is underneath everything, and science has shown us that everything is energy that just vibrates at different intensities. Your Essence has its own unique vibration, and it is affected by the energy surrounding it, like your clothing! Your Essence style is how you put together all the design elements that represent your Essence energy into the outfits you wear, to create an outfit that aligns, supports, enhances, and expresses the real you so others can truly see you.

Your Essence style may change as you grow and move into different times and places in your life, but your Essence never changes! Depending on the circumstances, we might find that we hide, even from ourselves, until we feel better. This is when we ignore our primary Type as not being our true Essence. We start behaving and hiding behind another Type. Most of the time it is the one that is closest to our primary. Sometimes, it just takes a little shift to place your primary Type back in front, so you can make choices based on its first! We are creatures of free will who can get caught up in not seeing our true selves because of our emotional state at the time. It is a big task to remember who you truly are at your innermost Essence. If you can, though, you will feel more empowered about yourself.

Inside us is a vast amount of truth and knowledge that is waiting to be tapped into. If we just touched upon a sliver of this from within, it would last a lifetime of adventure. The journey we take to learn and know about ourselves is the ultimate journey of growth. If we truly allow it to be an active part of how we learn to be with ourselves and others, I believe we will create a heart full of untapped, unconditional love waiting to be unleashed.

EMBRACING THE POWER OF YOUR PRESENCE

Embracing our own true power is the final step in finding unconditional love for ourselves. It is the true love of being present in a way that radiates unconditional love from within. When you are in this state of being, you feel a loving strength that keeps you focused on your true purpose in life. It becomes a desired state and goal in the process of all the growth we do in our life. Can we stay in this state of being all the time? No, we can't. There are so many moving parts to our life and emotions that we go in and out of every day.

Once you truly feel and understand what it is to embrace the power of your presence, you can tap into your internal strength for support when you need it. To learn the meaning of your Essence in terms of energy brings you closer to understanding your vibrational synchronicity with those around you, and those you want to attract. Then practicing, finding your unique Essence Formula, and creating your Essence Power Statement creates a tangible anchor to use until it becomes second nature. The steps I have taken you through in this book can be looked at as a journey to explore your true Essence at its depths and set it free. It is the letting go process that allows the conscious mind to see the true beauty of your own Essence and embrace it. Just like any practice, the more you do it, the easier it gets and the stronger you become.

I have written this book for several reasons and one of them, closest to my heart, is to help women to remember the strength we have within us, and to love ourselves with that strength. As women, we have a natural instinct to nurture and use our strength to help others, our family, our children. Nurturing our own Essence reminds us of this strength, and makes sure there is enough to give to others.

CHAPTER TWENTY

THE EMBODIED ESSENCE AND THE EMPOWERED PASSION

"Our hearts yearn to know who we are and why we are here. Have the courage to look for the answers."

—STEFFI JO

Cognitive psychologists examine how people think with both their minds and their bodies; this area of study is known as "embodied cognition." I believe that we also think with our spirit—the underlying way we accept information as if we intuitively know it is so. When people think with their minds, bodies, and spirits, it brings forth an authentic alignment and wholeness to our thinking. It is the feeling that you know, that you know, that you know, right down to your very existence. Thinking with your mind, body, and spirit is a way of being that I have named the Embodied Essence.

Dressing your Essence is an inner-play, an integration and visual representation of the mind, body, and spirit in material form and energy alignment as a whole. This results in a visual support of the Embodied Essence state of being. Embodied cognition experts state, "Our thought processes are based on physical experiences that set off associated abstract concepts, including those generated by the clothing that we wear. Clothing can enhance our experiences and our psychological states."

The publication *Positive Psychology News Daily* published an article called Enclothed Cognition. It shared that cognitive psychologists Hajo Adam and Adam Galinksy, from Northwestern University, have been examining the psychological and performance-related effects that wearing specific articles of clothing have on the person wearing them. They coined the term "enclothed cognition" for this phenomenon. Enclothed cognition captures the systematic influence that clothes have on the wearer's psychological processes. It is part of the larger field of research on embodied cognition. They found that the "clothing we wear affects our psychological states, as well as our performance levels. Given their findings, individuals can intentionally choose to wear clothing that will include more desirable psychological states and enhance task-related performance."

ENCLOTHED COGNITION AND ESSENCE

Here is where it gets even more interesting and fun: imagine with this scientific study in place and expanding on it with the knowledge of your own unique Essence qualities, you can consciously choose to wear clothing that aligns with your authentic core energy, your Essence. By doing so, you reach greater heights of authenticity in achieving your desired psychological states. It not only enhances your task-related performance, but you are claiming and owning your authenticity and allowing others to know the real you. You truly embody all of you in a way that others can visually perceive the real you! Imagine now what this knowledge can do for you, in your relationships with others, in your business, your personal and professional branding, in all areas where you know that when you expose your real, vulnerable authentic self, you attract what you desire. You develop your personal law of attraction in action and support your desires with purpose.

The study of enclothed cognition opens the door of understanding that what you wear can be a creative, non-verbal way to express your unique personality. However, it stops short of encompassing the knowledge of how and what to choose to show the real you. It is not just a choice of wearing clothing that is "right" for a situation; it is knowing all the elements that go into making choices that enhance your unique Essence and set you apart as a person that others truly get. It is that you are "authentic." You are a person who "walks her talk," you are the "go to" person, you are the one your audience wants to work with and be with. Put it all together and you truly embrace the power of your presence from the inside-out. This is the result of dressing your Essence.

ALWAYS EVOLVING

This is an ongoing journey. As you evolve, you might, all of a sudden, realize you are ready to upgrade from what you have been wearing as your Essence Formula. I remember when I first started dressing my Essence, I thought clothes with fifty percent of my Essence elements felt good enough to wear. I was overweight and unhappy with my body, and fifty percent was helping me feel better. I wore those clothes day in, day out and felt good about them, until one day I realized they were not helping me feel good about myself anymore. I outgrew the Formula. I was wearing outfits that had felt good and had helped for a long time, and as I started feeling better, I changed and realized that it was time to upgrade my Formula to match how I had evolved. It was evident when I would go shopping with my Essence Power Statement and could not duplicate the confident feelings I had before. It was time to upgrade my Essence Formula!

It was because I had evolved to become more in tune with my elements, and now my Essence craved something better, a higher level of alignment. I took all my fifty percent clothes out the door and over to the consignment store and started my new journey dressing in nothing less than sixty percent of my elements in my clothes, which supported my Essence so much more. I asked myself questions, did the exercises in this book again, took notes, experimented, and went shopping. I discovered I needed tweak my colors on the value scale. My Essence had not changed, but my stage of life and evolvement had, so I wanted to use my Essence in a new way. I was in a different emotional space and needed to adjust my Essence Power Statement to reflect that. Since then, I have shifted and evolved further, growing and becoming more of an expert in myself. Now, I don't feel good in anything less than seventy percent of my Essence elements.

You will get so in tune with your Essence when you work on it. Making it part of your everyday life, thinking about it every time you stand in front of your wardrobe, means you will make that shift, just like I did. You will feel good about yourself, get more confidence, and have less doubt about what to wear. As you grow in all of that, you will get a sense, a questioning, a wondering of, *What's next for me?* That feeling is a natural evolution. It's like when you exercise. If you start from nothing and try to do ten sit-ups a day, it will be hard. If you keep doing them, though, they will get easier and you'll become stronger and good at sit-ups. You will reach a point where your body tells your mind that maybe you could do more. It is not so much a conscious decision but a feeling. The mind listens to the body, reacts to what it is feeling, and asks more of itself. So, you try doing fifteen sit-ups, and once you have mastered that, you do twenty a day. You get stronger and keep progressing.

I have seen business women who do not evolve in how they dress their Essence, and all of a sudden, they are overlooked because they are not growing with the new times. Potential clients did not see them evolving, learning, and growing, so they could not imagine how these women could help them evolve, learn, or grow. These business women were not evolving, and it cost them new business. As feminine entrepreneurs, there is no question, we must be exploring and growing at all times; there is no staying still. This belief comes from the universal law: The Law of Change.

As a naturally evolving and questioning entrepreneur who wants to grow, you can use dressing as a tool to help you do that. You can keep dressing your Essence and using your enclothed cognition to do something much more than dressing. As we have seen, clothes go far beyond what is clothing, and dressing is not just dressing. It is understanding that you can allow others to see what is going on inside you and showing those changes as you grow allows others to see your authenticity.

THE EMBODIED ESSENCE

Embodied Essence is the result of self-awareness, self-acceptance, and self-love all coming together to embrace oneself with no judgment, no agenda, just for the sake of being alive in the moment and being a beacon for others to find their own way to wholeness. We tend to love pieces of us but the Embodied Essence is really about loving all of you, and understanding that you are not a collection of pieces, but are one whole person who should not be judged, by others or by yourself. You are the good, the bad, and the ugly, and it is all beautiful.

Embodied Essence is a level of awareness that you get to when you have consciously let go of learned behaviors based on belief systems from past experiences. Your decisions are made by checking in with all parts of you. Embodying your Essence is the wholeness of the experience that brings meaning of life to our existence. It is the one goal we seek that makes everything fall into place, to understand one's self and to love what we see, to love what we feel inside, our truth, and to have the courage to show ourselves with confident acceptance. This is when you fit in, into a world of authentic beauty, into a world starving for truth, love, and peace. When one person embodies her Essence, she becomes a light for others to follow their own path to self-love. Dressing your Essence helps others to find you.

Imagine knowing your Essence with a new understanding and applying your knowledge to everything you choose to do. In this book, I speak of dressing your Essence as the beginning to help you to see and feel who you are on the inside, so you may bring forth, with confidence, your authentic self on the outside. When you take this on in a conscious way, you take your life to the next level of achieving your desires. You become a conduit for change and growth. It is an attraction that is hard to resist for those who are waiting for you to show up and light the way for them to achieve the same. Learning to truly embody your Essence is a process that can be fulfilling. It opens your eyes to new ways to experience yourself.

Dressing your Essence is exciting because it makes being you so much more fun! It brings purpose and confidence to the choices you make when dressing and walking out your door. Living in the state of Embodied Essence is your higher, authentic version of yourself being who you came into this world to be. It is going through life in the child-like, innocent state of self-love, embracing who you were born to be in this world, loving it, and being grateful for it. There is a sense of freedom and freshness, being responsive to the richness and complexity of every moment from the innocence in which we came into this world. The mind is energized to take actions and get things done. Others can see and understand who your authentic self is from the inside-out.

BE DRIVEN BY EMPOWERED PASSION

Following on the heels of the Embodied Essence is the idea of Empowered Passion. Empowered Passion came into my thoughts and ignited a higher level through which we can honor the calling of the Essence. When you have embodied your essence, this next conversation flows naturally on, as you continue to step up. I believe all feminine entrepreneurs possess a mission or calling from their Essence—something that needs to be accomplished, no matter what. That mission is a driving force you cannot deny. It vibrates below the surface, refusing to be ignored, and won't allow you to rest until it is fulfilled. It is passion. When you empower that passion from the place of Embodied Essence, you give it a strength and confidence that fuels everything you do. Empowered Passion creates the next level of intensity in the mission that calls you from within.

This goes beyond the outdated idea of "following your passion." There is a lot of talk in the feminine entrepreneur's world of doing what you love to do, following your passion, working in your passion, but when you have embodied your Essence, that is not enough anymore. You sense your passion wants to become more powerful, so you are driven to empower it, and let it become your driving force, taking you to an explosive new level. You feel the need to shift into the passenger seat and give in to it. Hand it the controls and give it authority, because it is bigger than you, bigger than all of us. Allow your beingness and doingness to be driven by Empowered Passion.

This is also more than being an empowered woman. Empowered women are confident and in control, living with authority and freedom to do the things that call to them. An empowered woman knows her strength and isn't afraid to embrace it. Passion, though, is about an emotion so strong you can barely control it. When you bring empowerment to meet passion so strong, you get Empowered Passion. It means you are stronger and more successful in your enthusiasm, have control of your most powerful feelings, are aware of your capabilities, and are ready to take on even bigger dreams. Empowered Passion has a high vibration and an empowering impact on you and all those who surround you. It is felt, and it is seen in your presence. It is the thing that allows you to walk into a room and reveal the real you, every time, without even saying a word, because people feel you and your Empowered Passion. As a bonus, passion always trumps failure. Failures lose their power in the face of Empowered Passion.

Be driven by Empowered Passion! Turn everything over to it, so you can be at your highest level. This is the name of the game you must play today, as a feminine entrepreneur on a mission to grow your business. Aligning yourself with the high vibrations of your Empowered Passion, you will transform your journey in business and in life. It is a new world of entrepreneurs, and it is time to bloom into your next level of success! Do you have the courage to go there? Can you look within, beyond what you have experienced, seek the attributes you are made of, and apply them to everything you create? I believe you do, or you would not be reading this. I have given you a beginning, a door in, a way to peek inside and go through the door at your own pace, taking in as little or as much as makes sense to you. In dressing your Essence, only you can decide how much or how little you are willing to take on. Recognizing your embodied Essence is the process; owning it, living it, and being driven by Empowered Passion is the goal. Dressing your Essence is your declaration and a light for others to find their way; expressing your Essence is living it. Now, put on your Little Essence Dress, and go take on the world in your authentic Essence style!

CONCLUSION

THE JOURNEY CONTINUES

"When you have integrated all parts of yourself and embodied your alignment, as only you can do, you have truly embraced yourself in self-love."

—STEFFI JO

I hope that reading this book, following its exercises, and discovering your Essence are just the first of many steps along the path to embodying your Essence and empowering your passion. It is a wonderful, fulfilling, and enlightening journey, and I'm excited for you to continue upon it. This is the beginning, and there is more and more and more for you to discover! Below are some of the resources I mentioned throughout this book, which may help you explore further.

I also want to thank you for purchasing this book! To express my gratitude, I have added a special, hidden page on my website, just for you! On that page, I share a free gift to help in your journey of embodying your Essence. Find it at http://bit.ly/YourEssenceGift.

RESOURCES

Find The Online Quiz and More Information

Find the online Essence typing quiz and information about my upcoming programs and events on my website, www.expressyouressence.com.

Listen to The Feminine Essence Podcast

I share conversations with remarkable women who tell us of their personal journeys of transformation, growth, discovery, success, and stepping into the full expression of their unique Essence. Find it on your podcatcher of choice, or at http://bit.ly/EssencePodcast.

Social Media

Join me on social media on:

- Facebook at www.facebook.com/expressyouressence;
- Instagram at www.instagram.com/expressyouressence;
- Pinterest at www.pinterest.com/steffijoessence; and
- Twitter at www.twitter.com/essencecoach.

Take The Course

If you want to take this deeper, with guidance as you go through the process of undressing, connecting with, and dressing your Essence, take the Dress Your Essence course! It includes everything you need to continue along this journey, and truly express your authentic self in the way you dress. Find out more at http://bit.ly/DressEssence.

Read More About Beingness

These two books have profoundly influenced my understanding of Beingness.

- *Being and Time* by Martin Heidegger: http://bit.ly/MHeideggar_BT

- *Being-in-the-World* by Hubert L. Dreyfus: http://bit.ly/HLD_BeingW

Read More About Enclothed Cognition

Enclothed cognition is a fun and revolutionary subject. These two resources will help you understand it better.

- An introductory article from *Positive Psychology News* about enclothed cognition: http://bit.ly/ECognition

- A more in-depth report from the Journal of Experimental Social Psychology: http://bit.ly/EC_Journal

ABOUT THE AUTHOR

STEFFI JO

"If I were a flower,

I would grow in a place of sparkling sunshine.

The air would be clean and fresh,

With crisp mornings that awaken the earth.

There would be other flowers close by.

I would not be alone

In this abundant garden of beauty.

As the sun touched my mound of moist dirt,

I would feel unique as I spread my petals,

One by one,

for all to see.

How beautiful I would be,

If I were a flower!"

—STEFFI JO

One of my greatest passions is working with those women who are evolving into their next, most awesome version of themselves, and putting the pieces together to create from their authenticity, to be congruent in all areas of their personal and business lives. After more than 32 years owning and operating a traditional business, my life has led me to coaching and teaching my clients on how to truly see and understand their unique Essence, how to integrate all parts of who they are, and how to use this information when branding themselves and their business.

Not only have I created a long-standing business, but I am also an artist, and I have an acute sensitivity to the energy and vibration of the colors and design elements I use to express my heart on the canvas. I have blended all the parts of me into my passion for helping women to remember and trust in their unique beauty and wisdom.

My heart's drive, to help women, has come from my years of feeling disconnected from who I knew I was on the inside and what I was showing on the outside. I hid my true self as a child and through my teenage years and beyond, sometimes for survival and sometimes for acceptance. The experiences created one person I would show to others, and another one for myself. Through my own journey, I learned not to be afraid, and to just be me as whole person, accepted for who I am. I have grown from that journey and learned I can support that person on the inside and she can blossom on the outside. By knowing my Essence, I can be that confident, courageous, creative, wise, and loving woman on the outside!

To learn more about me, visit **www.expressyouressence.com.**

YOUR
ESSENCE
UNDRESSED
HOW TO DRESS YOUR CONFIDENCE
AND REVEAL THE REAL YOU!
STEFFI JO

www.ingramcontent.com/pod-product-compliance
Lightning Source LLC
Chambersburg PA
CBHW021142090426
42740CB00008B/892